Praise for *How to Be Great at Doing Good*

"Brendan Kennelly wrote, 'If you want to serve your age, betray it.' But what does it mean to betray your age? It means expose its lies, humiliate its conceits, debunk its arrogance, and question its certainties. Nick Cooney does this exquisitely. I would like his book to be in every school library and private bookshelf. But most importantly, I would like his words to be inscribed on the hearts of everyone who looks at the face in the mirror each morning and resolves to do all he can to make life better for the powerless. I am full of admiration for this young man."

—**Philip Wollen**, retired vice president, Citibank

"Too often, charity makes us feel good, but fails to do good. This timely, thoughtful book shows how our contributions can make a bigger difference."

—**Adam Grant**, Wharton professor and *New York Times* bestselling author of *Give and Take: Why Helping Others Drives Our Success*

"Nick Cooney is great at explaining *How to Be Great at Doing Good*, and I hope his book will be widely read. Even more important, though, is that its key ideas should be widely practiced. Then the results will be great, too—and Cooney and I agree that is what matters most."

—**Peter Singer**, Ira W. DeCamp Professor of Bioethics at Princeton University, author of *The Most Good You Can Do*, and one of *TIME* magazine's 100 most influential people

"Doing good is something we could all get better at. This book is the blueprint. Nick Cooney uses the same tools we use at OkCupid—math, logic, and analysis—but to an end that could benefit us all. If you're serious about making the world a better place, start here."

—**Christian Rudder**, co-founder of OKCupid and author of *Dataclysm: Who We Are When We Think No One's Looking*

"Impeccably written and extremely insightful. With eloquence and expressiveness, Cooney gives us a practical guide to examining our charitable efforts, measuring their efficiency, and maximizing their and our impact. If you've ever felt you could do more to make the world a better place, this book is for you."

—**Shushana Castle**, securities specialist, Sovereign Investments, and former board member of the Clinton Climate Initiative

"For anyone looking to make the world a better place, I highly recommend considering the arguments presented in *How to Be Great at Doing Good*. We're accustomed to trying to get the most for our money, but donating is the area where this principle is perhaps most important and least appreciated."

—**Holden Karnofsky**, co-founder and co-executive director, GiveWell.org

"Do you know that some charitable programs and organizations are thousands of times more effective than others (and not just because there are scams)? If you want to know who's doing the most good, this book will give you the tools to make accurate assessments. If you want to get the most bang for your buck, this book will show you the way."

—**John Robbins**, author of *Diet for a New America* and president of The Food Revolution Network

"Giving money to a social cause isn't merely a donation to charity; it's an investment. It won't yield a financial dividend, but the return on investment comes in the form of the kind of social change the investor wants to affect. Nick Cooney helps such philanthropists decide how they can get the biggest bang for their donated buck in this very worthwhile and clearly written book. Anyone interested in using his or her financial resources to help make the world a better place will be better off for reading it."

—**Paul Shapiro**, vice president, the Humane Society of the United States

"This book will challenge everything you've ever been told about what it means to do good. Whether you work or volunteer at a non-profit, or just donate to one, this book is going to change the way you think about charity. Most importantly, it's going to leave you with the power to make an even bigger impact on the world."

—**William MacAskill**, founder and director, The Centre for Effective Altruism, and author of *Doing Good Better*

"Wow, this is such a great book.... Don't waste another dollar or a moment of your time chasing wistful dreams; get focused and make the profound difference you long to see by reading (and enacting) Cooney's brilliant thesis."

—**Kathy Freston**, *New York Times* bestselling author of *Quantum Wellness* and *The Lean*

"Efficiency. Apply that word to charity work, and you're not just talking about saving dollars, but saving lives. In this book, Cooney expertly uses real-life examples to show how you can maximize your impact. Whether you donate to, volunteer at, or work for a non-profit, you need to read this book."

—**Jon Bockman**, executive director, Animal Charity Evaluators

"The world faces one big problem: Do-gooders rarely choose the most effective strategies to do good, and highly effective people rarely center their careers around doing good. Nick Cooney's book provides fascinating insights to address this problem, and thus to change the world."

—**Adriano Mannino**, chairman, Raising for Effective Giving

"Very well-written and remarkably well-researched, *How to Be Great at Doing Good* is a must-read book for anyone who's thinking about giving but needs a little help doing so."

—**Gene Stone**, *New York Times* bestselling author of *Forks Over Knives* and *Secrets of People Who Don't Get Sick*

How to Be Great at Doing Good

Why Results Are What Count and How Smart Charity Can Change the World

Nick Cooney

WILEY

Contents

Preface

Schindler's Regret

In 1936, a Czech citizen named Oskar Schindler enlisted as a spy for the secret intelligence service of the Nazi Party. Schindler was a banker and businessman and, although he was not German himself, his family had German roots. As the drums of war began to beat, fueled by the fiery speeches of Adolf Hitler and mass propaganda from the Nazi regime, Schindler went to work collecting information on troop movements and military installations in Czechoslovakia in preparation for a possible German invasion.

In July of 1938, Schindler was arrested by the Czech government and jailed for espionage. Had Germany chosen not to invade that country, the story for Schindler—and many others—may have ended there, in a dismal Czech prison. But just three months later Germany invaded and took control of large portions of the country. Schindler was sprung from his cell, praised for his work, and promptly sent on to Poland to continue his espionage in advance of another planned invasion.

A businessman at heart, Schindler wasn't content to merely pass the time in Poland taking notes and sending them on to the Nazi regime. So while there, he decided to also resume his life's main pursuit: making money. After searching for opportunities, Schindler came across an enamelware factory that had been put up for sale by a group of bankrupt Jewish businessmen. To Schindler, it seemed like a straightforward business opportunity. He would take over a failing factory and use his connections and experience to turn a hefty profit. That is exactly what Schindler did, earning an impressive income and living luxuriously in Poland for the next few years.

As World War II wore on, though, Schindler became disillusioned and eventually disgusted with what the Nazi Party was doing. The final straw for Schindler came in 1942 when the Nazis began to empty Kraków, a Jewish ghetto in Poland. Over a period of months the area's Jewish inhabitants were rounded up and shipped off to extermination or concentration camps elsewhere in Poland and Germany.

It just so happened that Schindler's enamelware factory was located not far from Kraków. In fact, a number of his workers lived there. Schindler, who was made aware of the planned action ahead of time thanks to his connections with the Nazi Party, was sickened by the thought of what was being done. The fact that it would be done to his own workers, people he saw every day toiling away at his factory, was more than he could stomach.

So Schindler, in his first act of secret defiance against the Nazi regime, had his Jewish workers start to sleep overnight at the factory in order to spare them from being rounded up and shipped off. His quick thinking saved the lives of his workers, and the experience left Schindler a changed man. From that point forward, the businessman who up until now had lived a life of luxury shifted his attention to a new goal: saving as many Jews as he could from the Holocaust that was underway.

Schindler began to employ more and more Jewish individuals as workers in his factory, not because he needed them (the overstaffing certainly cut into his profits), but because by doing so he could prevent them from being shipped off to extermination camps. Those added to the payroll included women, children, and the disabled, with Schindler assuring Nazi officials that all of them played important skilled roles in the manufacturing process. When those lies didn't succeed, Schindler used cash, diamonds, and luxury gifts he had obtained on the black market to bribe officials to allow him to continue hiring and retaining as many Jewish workers as possible. At its height in 1944, his factory "employed" over 1,000 Jewish workers.

As the war took a turn for the worse for Germany in 1944, the Nazi government decided that all German factories in Poland should be relocated inside the gates of the Polish concentration camps. Schindler knew that if his enamelware factory was moved inside a concentration camp, it would mean all of his Jewish workers would be forced to endure the brutality of the camp as well. So, once again using his cunning and the bribes that his wealth allowed, Schindler managed to talk his way into not only keeping his factory where it was, but also into being able to house hundreds of additional workers from other nearby factories at his plant.

A number of months later, as the Russian army began to advance on Poland, the Nazi government ordered Schindler's factory to close. Once more, Schindler used bribes and his skills of persuasion to obtain special permission to keep his factory open and have it moved to the German-controlled portion of Czechoslovakia. When, during the relocation process, several trainloads of workers were accidentally sent to concentration camps, Schindler used still more bribes of black market goods and diamonds to secure their release.

As part of the deal allowing him to keep his factory, Schindler had to agree to transition from an enamelware producer to a munitions producer and supply anti-tank grenades to the German war effort. Of course, this presented a major problem for Schindler. He didn't want to support the German war effort by producing grenade shells. But his hands were tied; had he refused, his factory would have been shuttered and his Jewish workers all shipped off to concentration camps.

So once more the crafty businessman turned to subterfuge. Schindler instructed his workers to produce only a very small number of useable artillery shells. When Nazi officials eventually caught wind that something might be amiss and came to question him about why he was producing such a small number of shells,

Schindler purchased pre-made shells from the black market and told officials they had been made at his own factory. It was enough to buy him the time he and his Jewish workers needed to ride out the end of World War II in safety.

By the time the War ended in 1945, Schindler had spent over one million dollars of his own money to protect his Jewish workers. Completely broke, he would go on to spend the remaining decades of his life running a series of failed businesses, dependent on financial assistance from Jewish organizations and from individuals whom he had saved during the war. Schindler's body now lies buried on Mt. Zion in Jerusalem beneath a tombstone that reads "The Unforgettable Lifesaver of 1200 Persecuted Jews."

Given the number of people he saved, we would expect that in looking back on what he had done Schindler would have, while no doubt horrified by the Holocaust that had occurred, at least been proud of his own actions and accomplishments. He had put himself at extreme personal risk. If high-ranking officials in the Nazi party had caught on to what he was doing, Schindler would undoubtedly have been executed. Furthermore, he had selflessly used up his entire fortune to feed and care for his Jewish workers and to bribe officials into allowing him to continue to keep them in his factory where they would be safe from harm. Thanks to his courageous work, he had saved over one thousand people from being murdered.

Yet, as the war ended, his work successfully completed, Schindler did not look back on what he had done with pride. In fact, he looked back on his work with another emotion entirely: regret.

Many of us are familiar with Schindler's story thanks to the blockbuster 1993 film *Schindler's List*, which depicts Schindler's heroic wartime actions. While fictionalized in some ways, the film is based in large part on extensive research and interviews with Jewish individuals who had been saved by Schindler.

At the conclusion of the film, Schindler laments to his close Jewish friend Itzhak Stern his regret about not having done more to help the Jewish people. While the dialogue used in the film is fictionalized, the sentiment expressed was one that Schindler truly felt: that he was in many ways a failure because he could have helped more people but failed to do so. The film's dialogue goes as follows:

> *Oskar Schindler:* I could have got more out. I could have got more. I don't know. If I'd just ... I could have got more.
> *Itzhak Stern:* Oskar, there are eleven hundred people who are alive because of you. Look at them.
> *Oskar Schindler:* If I'd made more money .... I threw away so much money. You have no idea. If I'd just ....
> *Itzhak Stern:* There will be generations because of what you did.
> *Oskar Schindler:* I didn't do enough!
> *Itzhak Stern:* You did so much.
>
> [Schindler looks at his car.]

> *Oskar Schindler:* This car. Göth would have bought this car. Why did I keep the car? Ten people right there. Ten people. Ten more people.
>
> [Removing Nazi pin from lapel]

> *Oskar Schindler:* This pin. Two people. This is gold. Two more people. He would have given me two for it, at least one. One more person. A person, Stern. For this.
>
> [Sobbing]

> *Oskar Schindler:* I could have gotten one more person ... and I didn't! And I .... I didn't!
>
> [Spielberg, 1994]

As courageous as he was, as skilled and cunning as he was, and as much as he sacrificed to save the lives of more than one thousand people, Schindler did not look back on his work with a feeling of pride and contentment. Instead, he looked back with regret.

Schindler—who certainly did so much—realized only too late that he had had the opportunity to save even more lives and failed to act on it. He realized too late that, had he thought more methodically, had he worked more smartly, had he been willing to sacrifice more of his personal comfort, many individuals condemned to death would have been able to live. As great a man as he was, this regret likely haunted him for the rest of his life.

You and I will probably never find ourselves in Oskar Schindler's shoes. We will probably never encounter the surreal, horrifying situation that Schindler faced in wartime Europe. But there is a profoundly important lesson that we can take from Schindler's experience, a lesson that should shape our own attempts to do what good we can in this world.

The majority of us are involved one way or another with charity work. Many of us donate to charity. Many of us volunteer our free time to support charitable causes. A few of us even work directly for non-profit organizations.

While Hollywood may never make a movie about you or me, the sobering reality is that the world we inhabit is much like the world Schindler inhabited. While we don't live in the midst of a genocide, and while we don't work alongside individuals who could be executed en masse at any time, we do live on a planet with a monumental amount of suffering, cruelty, and needless death.

We live in a world where tens of millions of people are imprisoned in slave-like conditions, the victims of human trafficking and labor bondage. We live in a world where tens if not hundreds of millions of people suffer acutely from easily preventable and easily treatable injuries and diseases. We live in a world where tens of billions of animals are confined and tortured in deplorable conditions on intensive factory farms. We live in a world where millions of elderly people live shut-in lives of piercing loneliness. We live in a world where human activity is poisoning or devouring huge swaths of the earth's ecosystems. We live in a world where hundreds of millions of women endure physical abuse, mutilation, or a denial of their most basic freedoms simply because of their sex.

But, as was the case for Schindler, we also live in a world where our money, our time, and our cleverness can spare dozens, hundreds, thousands of these individuals from misery—if we choose to use our money, time, and cleverness toward that end. That means that just as much hangs in the balance when we make our charity decisions as hung in the balance for Schindler when he took his wartime actions. Just as much hangs in the balance with whether we donate, how much we donate, and who and what we donate toward. Just as much hangs in the balance with how calculating we are in the charitable work we carry out, and with what programs our non-profit organizations choose to carry out. Just as much hangs in the balance with how hard we are willing to work, how smart we are able to be, and how focused we are on our goals. The suffering, well-being, and lives of so many individuals hang in the balance of our decisions, just as they did for Schindler's.

Because that is the world that we live in, Schindler's (dramatized) words should weigh as heavily on our minds as they weighed on his: "I could have got more out. I could have got more." Schindler looked back on his work not with pride but with regret. Regret for those whose lives he could have saved had he only been more calculating, more rigorous in his work.

If a man as courageous, smart, and committed as Oscar Schindler overlooked obvious opportunities to "get more out," then the question we must ask ourselves of our own charity work is this: What is it that *we* are missing? How can we "get more out" by being more calculating, more rigorous in our own work?

None of us wants to look back later in life with Schindler's regret, realizing only too late that, however much good we did, we could have done so much more. None of us wants to look back and realize that we could have helped more individuals but failed to do so.

This is a book about taking a calculated approach to doing good. It is a book about how to get more out of our donations, our volunteering, and the work that some of us put in as non-profit staffers. It is a book about how you and I can get more individuals out of a lifetime of misery.

This is also a book about why, like Schindler, we often fall short of our potential in the charity work we do. We'll explore the blind spots we have, the mistakes we make, and the self-defeating ideas we hold that prevent us from "getting more out." We'll learn how to identify these barriers so we can overcome them and succeed at truly changing the world for the better.

All of us have the potential to be great at doing good. All of us have the ability to achieve the sort of heroic results that Schindler achieved. All that's required is that we act with the intelligence and rigor that those who need our help most certainly deserve.

1

WHY CHARITY?

Asking Why

When I was eight, my brother, sister, and I had a little game we liked to play. The goal of this game was simple: to drive my mom crazy.

We had each received as a Christmas present a white magnetic board with a set of brown tiles. By arranging the tiles on the board you could write words or draw blocky, pixelated pictures. By today's standards this sounds like a pretty boring toy, but for us it was a lot of fun. On my brother's whiteboard he would use the tiles to spell out the letter "W." On mine I spelled out the letter "H." My sister spelled out "Y." Then we'd ask my mom a question—something innocent enough, like "What's for dinner?" After she'd reply, we'd each hold up our letters and chant, "Why?" The exchange went a little something like this:

"What's for dinner?"
"Pasta and green beans."
"Why?"
"Because that's what I'm making."
"Why?"
"Because that's what I bought at the store."
"Why?"
"Because that's what was on sale."
"Why?"
"Because that's what the manager made on sale."
"Why?"
"I don't know—now get out of my kitchen!"

"Why?"

"Because I said so!"

"Why?"

I think you get the point.

Obviously, we were just asking "why, why, why" to be annoying; there's always great fun in aggravating your parents. As adults though, the habit of continually asking ourselves "Why?" is one of the most important habits we can cultivate. As we dig deeper and deeper into things—into ourselves, into our beliefs, into how society operates—we come to greater understanding and a greater ability to live a more intentional life.

What do I want to accomplish before I die? How do I feel about marriage equality? Why do many people who are born into poverty remain in poverty as adults? For every such question there are both surface-level answers and deeper, more penetrating answers. Those latter answers can only be reached by repeatedly asking: "Why?"

Consider, for example, the following question-and-answer session you might have with yourself about poverty:

- "Why do many people remain poor into adulthood?"
- "Because they don't get high-paying jobs."
- "Why is that?"
- "Because they don't stay in school or go to college so they don't have the qualifications."
- "Why don't they stay in school or go to college?"
- "Well, one reason is they get bad grades so they become frustrated with it and drop out."
- "Why do they get bad grades?"
- "One reason is lack of parental involvement."
- "Why aren't parents as involved as they could be?"

Deeper and deeper we go. While there is rarely one single answer at the bottom, each time we ask "Why?" we move a little closer to understanding what's really going on.

All of us are used to at least occasionally asking: "Why?" Every one of us has had the experience of shifting our opinion on something after we learned or thought more about it. We want to understand the world around us, and we want to have good reasons for doing the things we do. That's the reason we ask others and ourselves that so very important question: "Why?"

The Goal of Charity

And that brings us to the "Why?" question at hand: Why do we do charitable things? To be more specific, why do we donate our money to non-profits? Why do we volunteer? Why do the founders of non-profits start those organizations? Why do non-profit employees do the work they do?

If someone were to ask us, we would probably all answer the same way: we do charitable things because we want to make the world a better place. We want to do good. Why do I donate or volunteer? I want to stop the spread of HIV, end torture, and support marriage equality. Why do non-profit leaders and employees file into work every day? They want to reduce overpopulation, fight climate change, provide clean drinking water to the poor, promote gender equality, protect animals from cruelty, and so forth. Whatever the specific work we do may be, at the heart of it lies the same noble goal: to make the world a better place.

Society as a whole has defined charity in much the same way. Pop open your Webster's dictionary and you'll see charity defined as "generosity and helpfulness, especially toward the needy or suffering," "aid given to those in need," and "public provision for the relief of the needy" (Merriam-Webster, 2014).

Boiling that dictionary definition and our common-sense understanding down, we see that charity has two key elements. First, charity is something we do to help others. It's not about satisfying our own desires. Second, the goal of charity is to reduce the suffering of those in need.

Not every action taken under the banner of charity has that exact goal. For example, some charitable work is not meant to help the needy per se, but rather to enrich the lives of those who are doing okay. Theaters, after-school programs, and Girl Scout troops do not exist to solve an acute problem, but rather to improve the lives of those they reach. Of course, improving well-being and helping those in need are two sides of the same coin. So perhaps a better way to define the goal of charity would be this: the goal of charity is to reduce the suffering and increase the well-being of others. To put that a little more simply, the goal of charity is to make the world a better place.

That definition still would not encompass every act that is dubbed "charity" in our society. Some religious congregants may donate to their church, not to make the world a better place, but because donating is what the Bible demands of them to reach heaven. Some environmentalists may donate to protect an old-growth tree, even though that tree can't suffer or experience happiness. Some people donate to non-profits, not because they think doing so will improve the world, but because doing so will help protect their own ability to hunt or own handguns.

While the IRS regards donations like these as charitable giving, they are outside the scope of both the dictionary definition of charity and what most of us consider true charity. When we think deep down about it, the goal of charity is not to benefit ourselves. The goal is to make the world a better place, one with less misery and more well-being.

Of course, a desire to help others isn't the *only* thing that drives the charitable decisions we make. We may have signed up for a charity run both because it raised money for a good cause and because it helped us get in better shape. We may have bought tickets to a fundraising gala both because we support the cause and because it was an opportunity to socialize with friends. While personal benefits like these can sometimes give us an added incentive to do good, at the end of the day our main goal is still an altruistic one. We really do want to make the world a better place.

Barriers to Good

That is, of course, a phenomenal goal. We should appreciate how wonderful it is that we have an impulse to help those in need. But despite our good intentions, we are not always as effective as we could be at reaching that goal. Blind spots, bad advice, personal biases, and other barriers are all around us, conspiring to prevent us from going very far toward making the world a better place.

Many books, magazine articles, and newspaper columns have been written about ostensibly charitable efforts gone terribly wrong. Sometimes these involve charities carrying out programs that do more harm than good, such as the World Wildlife Fund promoting legislation that could lead hundreds of thousands of animals to be lethally poisoned. Sometimes, charities squander vast sums of money, such as Yele Haiti, the Haitian relief organization founded by musician Wyclef Jean, which spent huge sums on celebrity plane tickets, personal payouts, and unfinished projects. Sometimes, organizations spend exorbitant amounts on overhead, such as the Cancer Fund of America, which spends over 80 percent of its income on fundraising.

Exposing bad apples like these is critically important, and we should tip our hats to anyone who does so. But that's not what this book is about. Because, as incompetent, counterproductive, or even criminal as some charities may be, our biggest barrier to doing good is not that we might be duped by a few bad organizations.

The biggest barrier is the set of mistakes that *all of us* make in our everyday charitable decisions. It is the critical flaws in approach and reasoning that plague even the most highly respected non-profits. It is the biases and lack of rigor that prevent us from accomplishing anything close to the amount of good we have the potential to accomplish.

Those missteps seem to stem from two main causes. The first is the fact that, as with many things in life, our perceived motivations as donors, volunteers, and non-profit workers are often quite different from our actual motivations. Our decisions are mainly driven by the crystal-clear objective embedded into our DNA over millions of years: look out for number one. Even when carrying out charitable work, our primary reward systems and concerns are often centered on ourselves.

The second reason our charitable efforts fall short of their potential is that we are taught charity is a warm, fuzzy thing and that as long as our intentions are good we should be applauded. We are not taught to think rigorously about our approach. We are not taught how to succeed at doing good, or even that success is what matters. So we aren't in the habit of making calculated decisions when it comes to doing good.

Over the course of this book, we'll take a closer look at what's holding us back in our efforts to make the world a better place. We'll learn how we can go around those barriers and make smarter charity decisions.

In Chapter Two we'll look at the difference between doing good and doing great. Instead of simply asking whether a certain charitable effort does good, we'll introduce a second question: How much good does it do?

In Chapter Three we'll examine, in the words of famed business author Jim Collins, the "brutal facts" about the relative impact that different charities and different charitable programs have on the world. Accepting these facts and allowing them to guide our charitable decisions is one of the most potent things we can do to achieve more good.

In Chapter Four we'll discuss how most non-profits—and most of us as individual donors or volunteers—fail to set a "bottom line" for our work. Setting a bottom line can bring increased focus to our charity work and enable us to do more.

In Chapter Five we'll talk about the importance of efficiency, or doing the most good for the least amount of money. For donors and non-profit staffers alike, efficiency is everything if we want to change the world.

In Chapter Six we'll consider why the amount of money a non-profit receives has virtually no relationship to how much good it does. We'll look at how we as donors can incentivize non-profits to become great and the barriers we face in trying to make smart donor decisions.

In Chapter Seven we'll discuss some of the ways in which our brains seem to hardwire us to make poor charity choices. We'll identify the biases that threaten to steer us off course and show how we can outsmart our brains and achieve our charitable goals.

In Chapter Eight we'll put the advice we've been given about charity our whole lives under the microscope. Being able to identify and weed out advice that sounds good but isn't true can help pave the way for intelligent charity decisions.

In Chapter Nine we'll explore our unwillingness to admit what we don't know, and our tendency to let assumptions guide our charity decisions. Testing those assumptions can help non-profits become a lot more successful.

In Chapter Ten, the final chapter, we'll review how to be great at doing good. We'll outline nine steps for making smart charity decisions and empowering ourselves to do far more good with the time, money, and energy that each of us has.

The Challenge of "Why?"

Why donate to this charity and not that one? Why carry out this program and not that one? Why work in this charitable field and not another one?

When it comes to talking about charity, "Why?" is often the elephant in the room. Politeness and hesitancy to critique the seemingly well-intentioned actions of others often prevents the question from even reaching our lips. Asking it seems to go against the spirit of charity. It could lead to hurt feelings. It could also lead to our own charitable actions being called into question, and if that happens, we might find ourselves at a loss for answers. If we are serious about making the world a better place though, there is nothing more important than asking that fundamental question of all charitable decisions: "Why?"

This little book is intended as a challenge. It is a challenge to get serious about charity. The challenge rests on two premises:

1. The first premise is that the goal of charity is to make the world a better place. It is to help those who are suffering and to increase well-being.

2. The second premise is that in whatever capacity you carry out charity—as a donor, a volunteer, or a non-profit worker—you want to succeed as much as possible.

If you disagree—if you think that the goal of charity is to benefit yourself or if you don't care how much your charity work actually improves the world—then this book won't be of use to you.

But if you do agree, then the challenge of this book, and the challenge of charity, is simple: keep those two premises in mind at all times, ask "Why?" of all charitable decisions, and follow that path where it leads you. It's a path that's sometimes uncomfortable and often surprising, but it's well worth the effort. The further along the path we go, the more power we'll have to truly change the world for the better.

2

DOING GOOD OR DOING GREAT?

A Tale of Two Charities

In 1953, a former U.S. Naval Reserve officer and newspaper editor named W. McNeil Lowery took a job at the Ford Foundation. Launched by Ford Motor Company founders Edsel and Henry Ford, the Foundation's noteworthy achievements have included providing initial funding for the creation of the Public Broadcasting System (PBS), helping launch the microloan movement of providing small loans to the global poor, helping launch civil rights groups like the Mexican American Legal Education and Defense Fund and the National Council of La Raza, and playing a major role in funding research to fight the AIDS epidemic.

But Lowery, whose personal background included contributing to and editing literary and theater journals, is credited with helping steer a portion of Ford Foundation funding toward a new area: the arts. After providing initial modest funding to orchestras and operas in the late 1950s, the Foundation distributed $6 million in grants to repertory theatres in 1962 and nearly $8 million in grants to major ballet organizations in 1963, with major gifts to support the performing arts continuing in the following years. By the time Lowery passed away in 1993, the Ford Foundation had become the largest non-governmental supporter of the arts in the United States. So crucial was Lowery's role in this shift that Lincoln Kirstein, co-founder of the New York City Ballet, called Lowery "the single most influential patron of the performing arts that the American democratic system has produced" (Anderson, 1993).

9

At the same time as Lowery began to direct millions of dollars toward theater, dance, and other performing arts organizations in the late 1950s and early 1960s, he became concerned about what he saw as a lack of cooperation and communication among such organizations. So in 1961 the Ford Foundation made a commitment to spend a quarter of a million dollars over the next four years helping to establish and launch a new non-profit called the Theatre Communications Group (TCG). The goal of TCG would be to improve communication between theaters and theater workers around the country so that they could learn from one another and bring the entire field of non-profit theater to greater levels of professionalism and success.

Fifty years later, the Theatre Communications Group still carries on that mission. Today TCG's operating budget hovers near the $10 million mark, and it has expanded its work into a range of areas: hosting national conferences and conducting research studies, providing $2 million in grants each year to individuals and theaters, publishing the works of hundreds of playwrights and other theater professionals, producing magazines and bulletins that serve as essential reading for those who work in or want to work in the theater industry, and advocating on Capitol Hill for increased federal funding of the theater arts.

By all appearances, Theatre Communications Group has met the goals set out for it by W. McNeil Lowery more than half a century ago. It has greatly improved communication between theaters around the country, helping elevate the professionalism of theaters large and small and helping launch the careers of many actors and theater professionals. In fact, in 2014 TCG was ranked as a top National Arts and Culture non-profit by the respected charity navigator Philanthropedia. This ranking means that experts in the arts and culture field rated TCG as one of the best in their class. In fact, out of all of the national arts and culture organizations that exist, these experts rated TCG as the third best in the country.

Earlier, we agreed that the goal of charity is to make the world a better place. We defined "making the world a better place" a bit more concretely by saying that the goal of charity is to help those who are suffering and to increase well-being. As we discussed, not every single act taken in the name of charity has these goals. But our common-sense understanding of charity and the dictionary definition both boil down to just that: work done to reduce suffering or to increase well-being.

With that in mind, let's pause for a moment to ask a question. Public praise aside, does the Theatre Communications Group succeed at the goal of charity?

Theatre Communications Group probably doesn't reduce much suffering. It's possible that by sharing information and resources it makes the lives of some theater professionals less stressful. It's possible that by helping more plays to be produced, driving more members of the public into theater seats, and thereby providing an enriching, thought-provoking, and entertaining experience to more people, it helps reduce the mild pain we all feel from the trials and tribulations of everyday life. It's possible that by exposing theater attendees to the moral lessons of plays, TCG might contribute in some small way to a more thoughtful society, which in turn could lead to a slightly more compassionate world. But it would be hard to make the case that, by increasing communication between theater professionals and providing additional funding for some theater programs, TCG is reducing a great deal of suffering in the world.

On the other hand TCG probably does increase well-being. For those who attend, the theater is often a very engaging, uplifting experience. Weaving together the powers of narrative and performance, great plays lead us to re-examine our lives, our relationships, and ourselves. They celebrate our shared experience: the joys of living and loving and the pangs of doubt, longing, and loss. Great plays can leave us spellbound, lost in contemplation, or laughing uproariously. Without a doubt, the theater enriches and improves our lives—and at times can even make us better people.

So does the Theatre Communications Group succeed at the goal of charity? Yes, it probably does. While it may not directly reduce much suffering, it does increase the well-being of those who attend the theater. TCG does indeed seem to succeed at making the world a better place.

Leaving the Theatre Communications Group aside for a moment, consider now a second charity.

In 1977, epidemiologist Larry Brilliant and public health specialist Girija Brilliant experienced something that people living a few generations earlier would never have thought possible: the end of smallpox. This disease, which dates back to around 10,000 BC and is estimated to have killed hundreds of millions of people in the 20th century alone, was eradicated over a 200-year span as smallpox vaccines began to be implemented first in Europe and the United States and then around the world. The last known case of naturally occurring smallpox was diagnosed in Ali Maow Maalin, a hospital cook in Somalia, on October 26, 1977. In 1980, after years of intense verification work, the World Health Assembly of the United Nations declared that smallpox was officially eradicated.

Larry Brilliant, whom *Wired* magazine dubbed "humanity's best hope against the next pandemic," had led the World Health Organization team working to eradicate the disease in South Asia in the 1970s (Williams, 2014). His wife Girija also worked there as part of the WHO team. With the eradication effort completed, the husband and wife pair was faced with a new question: What should they do next? With smallpox gone, what was the best way they could continue to be of service?

Eventually they connected with Govindappa Venkataswamy ("Dr. V"), an esteemed Indian eye surgeon who had just launched an aggressive effort to combat and reverse blindness in India. Curing blindness may sound like science fiction, but it's not. Of the estimated twelve million blind people in India, 80 percent have lost their vision due to cataracts. These cataracts can be removed (or prevented) through a simple and inexpensive surgical procedure, thereby curing people of blindness.

Dr. V's goal was to do for eye care what McDonald's had done for hamburgers: create a chain of clinics around India that used hyper-efficient, assembly-line processes to carry out a huge number of cataract surgeries quickly and at low cost. This chain of clinics, known as Aravind Eye Care Systems, now performs over 200,000 eye surgeries a year. Revenue earned from the one-third of patients who can afford to pay allows the chain to provide free services to the two-thirds of patients who cannot.

Recognizing an opportunity to do great good by providing financial support for Dr. V's work, Larry and Girija Brilliant launched the Seva Foundation in 1978. Its first donor, and a major early supporter, was a then relatively unknown computer programmer named Steve Jobs. (Jobs would later go on to start the iconic computer and phone company Apple.) Seva reports that, since 1978, it has helped a whopping three million people regain their eyesight by funding simple eye surgeries, first in India with Dr. V, and now in more than twenty countries around the world.

While the Seva Foundation is not rated on Philanthropedia, it does receive a very high score from Charity Navigator, another popular website that ranks and rates non-profit organizations. As far as size goes, Seva's annual budget had hovered around $3 million per year until 2013 when it jumped up dramatically to $9 million.

Let's now ask of Seva the same question we asked earlier of the Theatre Communications Group. Does Seva succeed at the goal of charity? In other words, does the organization actually make the world a better place?

It certainly seems that way. In the past year alone, Seva prevented or cured blindness in more than 100,000 people in impoverished countries around the world, completely sparing those individuals from the daily misery of blindness and dramatically increasing their own and their families' well-being. As was the case with the Theatre Communications Group, it certainly seems that the Seva Foundation is succeeding at the goal of charity—making the world a better place.

Now that we've learned a bit about both TCG and Seva, imagine yourself in the following scenario.

It's December 28. The holiday season is mostly over, but you're still reveling in that long stretch of time off (or partly off) that lasts through New Year's Day. Sitting at the kitchen table that evening, mug of hot chocolate in your hand, you tear open two envelopes that have arrived for you that week and pull out the paper contents inside.

The first letter is from a non-profit called the Theatre Communications Group. After explaining all of the great work they do to support theaters, theater professionals, playwrights, and actors, they ask you to make a special year-end contribution to help them continue their important work. There's a postage-paid return envelope and a pre-printed return form all ready to go; all you need to do is enter your credit card information or write a check and drop the envelope in a mailbox.

You start to consider their request, but before coming to a decision you open the second envelope. This one is from a non-profit called the Seva Foundation. After explaining all of the great work they do to help prevent and cure blindness in India, Nepal, Bangladesh, and other countries, they ask you to make a special year-end contribution to help them keep up their important work. There's a postage-paid return envelope and a pre-printed return form all ready to go; all you need to do is enter your credit card information or write a check and drop the envelope in a mailbox.

You're feeling in a particularly charitable mood, so you start to seriously consider both requests. Work has gone well this year, and you have $1,000 you feel you could spare for a good cause. Plus it will be a nice little tax write-off if you get it in the mail before the year ends.

You decide that you will go ahead and donate that $1,000. But which organization should you donate to? Should you donate it all to Seva? All to the Theatre Communications Group? Maybe you should split it down the middle, with $500 going to each charity. Maybe you should donate $800 to one and $200 to the other.

The options are there on the table. What would you do?

Doing Good, or Doing a Lot of Good?

If the measure of success for charities is an up or down vote on whether they are making the world a better place, then we could probably say that both the Theatre Communications Group and the Seva Foundation are succeeding. While their areas of focus are very different, both of these charities are making the world a better place.

But if we want to be great at doing good—and if we want the charities we support to be great at doing good—then we need to rely on more than just a thumbs up or thumbs down approach. The fact is that almost all of us intuitively take a more thoughtful approach than this. We don't just ask ourselves "Does this do any good?" We also ask, "*How much good* does this do?"

Imagine that you're reading a newspaper article about a group in your community called Save Our Kids, which works to remove children from abusive households. You happen to be a donor to Save Our Kids—at some point you signed up for their email list, and just last week you made a $50 donation to the group on its website. So you read on with interest, and learn that Save Our Kids raises around $1 million a year from donors like you.

Then you read that for all the money they receive, Save Our Kids has only rescued one child from an abusive household in the past year. "A million dollars a year to protect one kid?" you think to yourself, rather annoyed and a bit shocked at how little the group has done. "I'm glad that kid is safe, but is that really the best they can do for a million dollars? That's the last time they get a donation from me."

On the thumbs up or thumbs down scale we were using earlier, Save Our Kids would still get a thumbs up—after all, it did make the world a better place by helping one child. But you'd be rightfully annoyed that so little was accomplished with so many resources. It's very understandable that you would no longer want to donate to that particular group.

But now let's change the scenario a little bit. Imagine instead that you read that Save Our Kids has actually rescued 1,000 children from abusive households in the past year. How would that make you feel? You'd probably feel pretty good about Save Our Kids, and pretty good about yourself for donating to them. Next time the group asked you to donate, you'd probably donate even more than last time.

The point is that, for most of us, the goal of charity isn't just to do any good at all. We want our charity work to do *a lot* of good. Saving a child from abuse? That's good. Saving 1,000 children from abuse? That's GREAT. In fact, if we want to get technical, that's a thousand times better than saving just one child from abuse.

Of course, this is only true if our goal is, in fact, to make the world a better place. It is only true if the reason we donate, volunteer, and do other charity work is, in the words of the Merriam-Webster Dictionary, to provide "helpfulness, especially toward the needy or suffering."

On the other had, if our goal was just to do a good deed—in order to feel proud of ourselves, to live up to social expectations, to get into a heaven, or for some other reason that revolves around us—then it doesn't really matter whether our donation helped one child or whether it helped 1,000 children. All that matters is that we did something we consider to be good. Whether it improved the world a whole lot or improved the world only a tiny bit doesn't matter to us.

If you've made it this far in the book though, you've already agreed that charity is not about benefiting yourself; it's about helping others. You've also already agreed that you want to succeed as much as possible at improving the world. So for you and me, and more importantly for abused children themselves, our earlier conclusion remains true. Sparing 1,000 children from abuse is a whole lot better than sparing one child from abuse. In fact, it's a thousand times better.

Think back to Oskar Schindler and the profound sense of regret he felt as World War II ended. He had succeeded at saving 1,200 Jewish individuals from torture and certain death at the hands of the Nazi regime. But he knew that saving 1,300 Jewish individuals would have been even better—100 more people could have been spared a grisly fate. Schindler's regret came from knowing that he could have saved those additional lives, he could have "got more out" had he gone about his work more thoughtfully.

Rather than simply considering whether a non-profit does some good, the more important question to ask is *how much* good it does. If we want to be great at doing good—if we want to improve the world as much as possible—then this is the question to ask of all our charitable actions. It's the question to ask when deciding between a donation to the Seva Foundation, the Theatre Communications Group, and any other non-profit. It's the question to ask when deciding which organizations to volunteer with and what work to carry out.

If the goal of charity is to make the world a better place, then this follows: individual charities succeed to the extent that they make the world a better place. Great charities improve the world a whole lot. Mediocre charities improve the world a moderate amount. Bad charities improve the world only a little, or make the world even worse off than before.

What exactly does all this mean for Seva, TCG, and where our year-end donations should go? To answer that question, let's take a short detour to an unlikely place: a ski lift at the top of a snow-encrusted Arizona mountain.

3

FACING THE "BRUTAL FACTS" ON HOW MUCH GOOD WE ARE ACCOMPLISHING

Gritting Our Teeth and Heading Down the Slope

A few years ago I went skiing for the first and possibly the last time in my life. It was one of the most unpleasant experiences I've ever had.

The debacle took place 9,000 feet up in the White Mountains of eastern Arizona. While the idea of skiing in Arizona may sound like a joke, or at least something entirely unnatural (maybe you're imagining artificial snow packed on top of hot, dusty cliff sides, with a cactus poking out from beneath the white façade), the reality is that the White Mountains are pretty aptly named. They are hit with 250 inches of a snow a year, more than enough to make the area a skiing Mecca for those living in the southwestern United States.

Something you should know about me is that I have moderate phobias of heights and speed. I'm one of those people who can't stomach roller coasters or any amusement park rides that go very high or very fast. Ferris wheels are okay, although still scary. You can pretty much forget about trying to get me on any rides more intense than that. Part of the fear is that I don't like the feel of being physically out of control. While I don't have bad dreams very often, when I do, one of the most common scenarios is I'm driving a car downhill and the brakes suddenly stop working.

Okay, you get the point. So now picture me skiing for the first time, sliding down a mountain at an ever-increasing speed with just an hour or so of training to get me started. It was pretty bad. Things became really unpleasant when I got on the wrong ski lift and accidentally ended up at the top of a mountain—alone and with no way to get down other than on my skis. I did manage to make it down (falling at least a dozen times in the process, with a couple really big wipeouts), but it was one of the scariest things I've ever experienced.

That night I lay in bed unable to fall asleep. Every time I closed my eyes I suddenly found myself at the crest of a massive hill, about to hurtle downward with no way to stop the momentum. Fear—of heights, of being out of control, of hurtling faster and faster down the mountain—had taken over my brain. It took five hours before I could finally distract myself enough to drift into sleep.

How can we make the world as much of a better place as possible with the limited time and money that each of us has? How can we become great at doing good?

It seems like a simple question. But answering it honestly is like staring down the slope of a mountain. Once we start moving in that direction, it can be hard to stop. And once we start to go down that path, we might quickly find ourselves, and our views on charity and what it means to do good, a very long way from where we started.

Naturally then, we're going to be very hesitant to dig in our poles, grit our teeth, and start heading down that slope. The psychological reality of being human is that we hate to change our opinions and our behaviors, even when those changes would do a lot of good for the world. Asking "Why?" of all charitable efforts would compel us to do both of those in an area of our lives that we think should be easy and all about feeling good.

But there's no way we can become great at doing good if we aren't willing to go down that mountain. There's no way we can, in the words of Oskar Schindler, "get more out" if we aren't willing to ask the hard questions, accept the hard answers, and pivot accordingly.

In the business classic *Good to Great*, author Jim Collins and his research team examined decades of stock data to see which factors distinguished good companies from great companies. Good companies were defined as those whose stock price performed about average for their industry for several decades. Great companies were defined as those whose stock price was roughly on par for their industry for at least fifteen years, but which then experienced a dramatic upswing in share price that lasted at least fifteen years.

Among the five key differences that Collins and his team found between the great companies and the merely good ones was this important one: great companies were willing to "confront the brutal facts" of trends in their industry and to change their approach when needed, sometimes dramatically so. Companies that were merely good, as well as those that ultimately failed, were unwilling to accept the "brutal facts" as true. They ignored or downplayed information that suggested they needed to make serious changes, choosing instead to stay their previous course. Ultimately, both they and their shareholders paid the price for their reluctance to face hard truths (Collins, 2001).

Collins presents an example of two major grocery chains, A&P and Kroger, who both faced a similar dilemma in the 1970s. The old model of the grocery store was fading away. Customers now preferred to shop in large supermarkets with delis, pharmacies, and other conveniences. While Kroger embraced the new trend head on, investing a great deal of money to expand and upgrade their stores, A&P resisted. Their current model, which relied on a simple store layout and prices kept as low as possible, had worked for decades. Despite what the market trends suggested, A&P clung to the belief that their approach would continue to work as long as they kept prices extremely low.

In the ensuing years, Kroger thrived while A&P floundered and was eventually taken over by another chain. Kroger had been willing to confront the brutal fact that it would have to make major changes to meet consumer demand. A&P, emotionally tied to a strategy it was comfortable with, was unwilling to face reality. That difference led one chain to succeed and the other to fail.

All Charities Are Not Created Equal

Earlier we agreed on two premises. First, that the goal of charity is to improve the world by reducing suffering and increasing well-being. And second, that we want our charity work to succeed as much as possible.

If we accept those premises and act on them, we will eventually come face to face with some "brutal facts" about the world of charity. As was the case with the for-profit companies Collins examined, how willing we are to face the sometimes unpleasant and unexpected realities of charity work will determine in part how successful we are at doing good. Are we willing to pivot, sometimes drastically, in response to those facts? Or will we find reasons to ignore them, discount them, and continue doing things in more or less the same way we had before? One of the hard facts about charity that we need to confront leads us back to the Theatre Communications Group, the Seva Foundation, and what it means to succeed at doing good.

The hard fact is this: there is a massive difference in impact among charities in different fields. And that difference has nothing to do with how intelligent, skilled, or caring the staffers at those charities are.

While we agreed that both TCG and Seva probably improve the world, there is a vast difference in *how much* each of them improves it. The Theatre Communications Group increases communication between theater professionals and provides grants to theaters and individuals. The Seva Foundation prevents or cures blindness in over 100,000 people each year. Nearly all of us would agree that preventing or curing blindness is a dramatically greater good than boosting the quality of the theater arts field. I imagine that most of us would say that restoring sight to even a small number of people is a greater good than boosting the quality of the theater arts field.

And that means that—in our ethical worldview—Seva is a more successful charity than the Theatre Communications Group. That is, it accomplishes the goal of charity to a larger degree than TCG does. It's like when we compared saving 1,000 children from abuse to saving one child from abuse. While both do good, Seva does (in most of our opinions) more good. It does more to make the world a better place.

So if we are sitting at our kitchen table with a mug of hot chocolate, trying to decide whether to send a $1,000 check to Seva, to TCG, or to split the money between the two of them, the answer is clear. If our goal is to make the world a better place, and we want to succeed as much as possible at doing that, we should make the check out to the Seva Foundation.

The fact that one of these two organizations is more successful than the other at making the world a better place should not be surprising. Any time we compare two different organizations, one is inevitably going to be more successful. Compare two for-profit companies and one will inevitably be more profitable than the other. Compare two major league baseball teams and one will inevitably have a better record. Sometimes two teams, two companies, or two non-profits are so close that it's hard to tell which one is really more successful. But usually the difference becomes clear if we take the time to look for it.

While it may not be a surprise that one of our non-profits seems more successful than the other, something is surprising: the incredibly massive difference between the two of them. Seva isn't just moderately more successful than TCG at making the world a better place. It is probably *over a thousand times* more successful.

How can we tell that the difference between the groups is so large? How can we even compare the impact of two non-profits whose areas of work are so different?

Asking the Genie in the Bottle: Making Comparisons When Comparisons Seem Hard

Initially, we might think that a comparison like this—looking at two charities in unrelated fields to determine which does more to improve the world—just isn't possible. If that's how you feel, or if you're not certain you agree that Seva is more successful at improving the world than the Theatre Communications Group is, consider the following.

Imagine that you're on your way home from work and a genie suddenly appears in the passenger seat of your car. He has the big blue body, the white hat, and a little magic lamp down below. He really fits the genie stereotype, at least until he opens his mouth.

"Greetings," he says. "I am the genie of the magic lamp. But I am not an ordinary genie who will grant whatever wish you happen to have. I am the Charity Genie, and I am here to grant you one of two possible wishes for making the world a better place. You pick which one you want to come true, and with a snap of my fingers I will make it true."

Without letting you get a word in edgewise, he continues. "First, we have wish number one. If you choose this wish, you will instantly restore sight to 100 poor blind people. Next up, we have wish number two. If you choose this wish, you will instantly improve communication between theater groups and provide grant funding to dozens of theaters around the country."

"Well," he says, "Which one will it be? Hurry up, I haven't got all day!"

Which one would you pick: Wish one or wish two?

If you're having trouble deciding, try picturing your friends and family members as the beneficiaries of each wish. Imagine that you have 100 friends and family members who have gone blind—and with wish number one you could bring their sight back. Next imagine that all of those friends and family members work in the theater industry and attend plays regularly. With wish number two you could provide them more grant money, improve their communication with one another, and increase the quality of their productions.

Which one would you pick?

Personally, I'd go with wish number one. I'd much rather have 100 people spared from blindness than improve the quality of the theater arts, especially if it were my friends and family members who stood to benefit. Don't get me wrong, I love the theater and attend it regularly. I think it would be wonderful if more plays were put on, and if plays were of a higher caliber. But sparing 100 people from blindness just seems to me to be more important than helping to improve the theater arts. It seems to do more to help those who are in need, and more to improve well-being. It seems like a greater good. In fact, even if the first wish spared just ten people from blindness, I'd probably still choose it.

It appears that I'm not alone in choosing wish number one. A straw poll conducted online of several hundred people found that 97 percent of them would rather spare 100 people from blindness than improve the quality of the theater arts through better communication and millions of dollars in grants.

If you, too, chose wish number one, that means that, even if Seva only cured 100 people of blindness per year, you would still think it was a more successful charity than the Theatre Communications Group. (If you chose wish number two, how many people would Seva need to cure of blindness before you would choose wish one? Consider it for a moment and decide where you would draw your own line in the sand.)

Of course, the Seva Foundation doesn't just restore sight to 100 people per year. It restores sight to *more than a thousand times* that amount, over 100,000 people per year. That means that in our ethical worldview—the majority of us, those of us who chose wish number one—the Seva Foundation does *at least a thousand times more good for the world* than the Theatre Communications Group. Seva is at least a thousand times more successful than TCG at achieving the goal of charity. For someone like me, who would rather spare just ten people from blindness than improve the quality of the theater arts, I'd have to conclude that Seva is *ten thousand times* more successful than TCG at improving the world.

So here we have two charities of similar size, both highly praised by the most popular charity advisor websites, and both with a very positive public reputation. Yet by most of our estimations, one of them does at least a thousand times, and maybe even ten thousand times, more good for the world than the other.

What does this mean for us as potential donors and volunteers to these organizations? It means everything!

It means that, on average, donating just $100 to Seva would probably do more good for the world than donating a whopping $100,000 to the Theatre Communications Group. (Seva does over a thousand times more good than TCG. So donating $100 to Seva does more good than donating $100 × 1,000 = $100,000 to the Theatre Communications Group.)

For someone like me, who thinks that sparing even ten blind people is more important than improving the theater arts, I'd have to conclude that donating $100 to Seva would probably do more good for the world than donating $1 million to TCG.

It would also mean that spending just a single hour of time volunteering with Seva would probably do more good for the world than spending *six full months* (and for me, *six years*) of non-stop, forty-hours-a-week volunteering with TCG.

Those are incredibly large differences. Prior to thinking about it here, would any of us have expected that supporting one charity could have that much more of an impact than supporting another?

There Are Always Big Differences Between Charities

You may not agree that sparing 100 people from blindness is a greater good than improving communication between theater professionals. Maybe you don't think going blind is that bad. Maybe you think that improving the quality of theaters dramatically improves the world.

Regardless of what your exact values are, one overarching point remains true. When you compare charities in different fields, you will find massive differences in how successful each is at achieving the goal of charity.

Admittedly, comparing an arts organization like TCG to a hyper-efficient human health charity like Seva is kind of like putting a high school boxer in the ring with Mike Tyson at his prime. It's going to be a knockout. But I chose to spotlight those organizations for two reasons.

First, there is a massive amount of donor money going to the arts world each year. In 2013 Americans gave $14.4 billion to arts and culture organizations. This is more than half the amount given to support public health. It is close to double the amount spent on protecting the environment and animals combined, even though we live in an era when environmental destruction and animal abuse are occurring on scales unprecedented in human history. So it's important that we understand the value of donating to arts organizations relative to what other good we could accomplish with our money.

Second, comparing TCG and Seva illustrates just how incredibly different non-profits can be in terms of impact. One charity can be tens, hundreds, thousands, even tens of thousands of times more successful than another at making the world a better place. While the difference in our example is particularly vast, there will often be large differences between charities that both—at first blush—seem like good charities. You might find, when you crunch the numbers, that in your view the Nature Conservancy does fifty times more good for the world than the Boy Scouts of America. Population Services International may do two-hundred times more good for the world than Susan G. Komen for the Cure. Although Seva and the Theatre Communications Group are particularly far apart in terms of impact, we could have picked any two charities at random and probably would have found a big difference in how successful each one is at making the world a better place.

Note that this has nothing to do with the professionalism of each organization or the quality of the people who work there. The Theatre Communications Group and the Seva Foundation may have equally low overhead and an equally skilled board of directors. They may be equally transparent about their financials and equally skilled at engaging volunteers. For all we know, the staff at TCG and Seva are equally talented, selfless, passionate, and dedicated people.

But when it comes to accomplishing the goal of charity, making the world a better place, Seva is vastly more successful than the Theatre Communications Group. The very type of work that TCG has chosen to do dictates that it will never be very successful at achieving the goal of charity. The same holds true for many other charitable organizations. No matter how smart, talented, and passionate you may be, you cannot reach past the bounds your field imposes on you.

That's why it's vitally important to think carefully about what type of charity work to support or to carry out. For the average donor and volunteer, this is one of the two most important decisions you'll ever make. It will mean the difference between being able to do a tiny bit of good and being able to do a huge amount of good.

(The other most important decision is which specific charity to support. Once you've decided to focus on, say, population planning, the next question is which specific population planning charities to support. We'll talk more about that in the next chapter.)

If we truly want our charitable work to succeed—if we want to improve the world as much as possible—then we must start by figuring out what type of charity work will allow us to do that.

Accepting the Fact That We Can Always Do Better

In comparing Seva and the Theatre Communications Group, we ended up uncovering some pretty "brutal" facts. They are "brutal" in that they will be very hard for staff members, donors, and volunteers of the Theatre Communications Group to hear and accept. They are also "brutal" in how they lay bare the huge difference in impact between these two organizations and the hugely different results you would obtain from donating to or volunteering with one group instead of the other.

They have also very clear implications for donors and volunteers. Donors to TCG who want to not just "do good" but improve the world as much as possible will need to shift their donations from TCG to Seva or another similarly high-impact organization. Psychologically, this can be a very tough shift to make, especially for those who are big fans of the theater or who have been supporting TCG for years.

Most of us do accept we could be doing things better and make changes when those changes are very small. For example, a TCG donor who realizes he or she could do more good by making a dedicated donation to TCG's High School Theater Support Fund (a fictitious program I'm inventing here), instead of making a general donation to TCG as they have in the past, will find it fairly easy to make that switch. But when the facts suggest we should make big changes, we find that incredibly difficult to accept.

If I were a donor to the Theatre Communications Group, my instinct upon reading the last few pages would be to try to find justifications for why—despite those facts—I should keep doing what I've been doing, namely donating to TCG. The idea that my money could have done more good if donated elsewhere is threatening. It means that I may have been—gulp—not perfect in making my decision! It means that I may have done less with my money than I could have. None of us wants to feel this way, whether we're talking about charitable donations or anything else.

But if we want to become great at doing good, we need to have the same willingness to accept the "brutal" facts and act on them as the successful companies profiled in Collins' book had. Being great at doing good requires an earnest willingness to realize that there is always something better we could be doing—we just don't know what that is yet.

While it takes healthy doses of maturity and humility, we should try to view whatever hard facts we come across not as threats but as opportunities. Because opportunities are exactly what they are. Every "brutal fact" that shows we could be doing charity in a better way presents us with an exciting new opportunity to do more good for the world! It presents us with an opportunity to "get more out"—to help more people, to reduce more suffering, to make the world an even better place.

So rather than be afraid of hard facts, we should crave them. They may not do great things for our egos. But if we act on them they will do incredible things for the world around us, and for those we want to help.

It's Always Subjective, and There's No Way Around That

The reality is that comparing charities is always going to be subjective. Our conclusions are going to vary based on our own personal ethical worldviews. We don't live in an intricately ordered, universe-sized video game where every positive change we can bring about is assigned a specific number of "good points." So when comparing the impact of restoring sight to improving theater communication (or comparing the impact of feeding a homeless person to painting a mural on a public building; or comparing the impact of protecting an acre of wild land to preventing one person from contracting HIV), we have no choice but to make our own ethical judgments.

As a result, my estimations of how two charities compare will sometimes be different from yours, and yours will sometimes be different from your neighbor's. Such differences are inevitable in a world where each person has his or her own political, social, religious, philosophical, and ethical belief systems. Estimations of how much good a charity does for the world will never have the precision of a baseball team's win-loss record or a company's statement of net revenue. In charity, measurements will always be subjective, not objective. That's just how it has to be.

A few people may argue that, since there's no way to objectively compare charities, we shouldn't bother comparing them at all. But that sort of thinking would be at odds with how we all act in our daily lives.

Consider, for example, the question of whom to date or marry. Like comparing charities, comparing potential romantic partners is complex, uncertain, and subjective. It's subjective because who you choose depends in part on your values, your personality, your tastes, and so forth. Yet here we don't throw up our hands in defeat and say there's no way to compare potential partners. We don't decide that, because our judgments will always be subjective, we shouldn't even bother trying to pick a great partner. If that were our approach, coupling would be pretty easy. We would just walk down the street and choose whomever we happened to pass first—regardless of sex, age, and any other characteristics—as our lifelong partner.

Of course, that's not how we do it. We may not be able to predict the single best match for us, but—using our own subjective judgment, plus reasoning—we can and do rule out at least the 95 percent of people we know are not good matches for us. The same general approach applies to choosing a profession, deciding who to vote for, and many other decisions we make. Despite these being ultimately subjective questions, we compare and contrast and use reasoning to make our best guesses. We're not always right, but we usually end up with a much better match than we would have if we just chose at random.

The same is true when comparing charities. Will our estimates of how two charities compare always be right? Certainly not. Our estimates will also probably shift over time as we learn new information. But using our judgment and reasoning to make these estimates will allow us to do far more good than simply picking charities at random. It will allow us to do far more good than simply sticking with whatever charities we support now, or supporting charities that we just happen to have a personal connection with.

And guess what? We *already* make judgments about which charities are better or worse than others. If we didn't, why would some of us choose to donate to Greenpeace and not a local Tea Party chapter? Why would some of us choose to donate to the NRA and not the ACLU? Why would some of us choose to support hunger relief charities and not Mormon evangelism efforts?

All of the charity decisions we make right now are in part the result of a quick mental calculus on how much good we think a particular charity does. All that I'm advocating is that we be more rigorous in making these decisions—that we turn intuitive mental calculations into quantified pen-and-paper calculations. Because when we do, as we did with Seva and the Theatre Communications Group, we will sometimes be shocked by what we find.

Does doing this require some extra work? Of course. But think how much time we put into other serious decisions in our lives, decisions where *we* stand to gain or lose. The average American does about twenty hours of research and comparison-shopping before buying a new car. How many of us spend the same amount of time researching and comparison-shopping before choosing which charities to support? The fact is that our charity decisions are far weightier than our decision of whether to go with a Nissan Altima or a Toyota Corolla. There is a lot more at stake. Unfortunately though, when it's *others* who stand to gain or lose and not us, we don't feel the same intrinsic motivation to put in the legwork needed to make a good decision.

If we want to become great at doing good, we need to put in the effort that's required. When we're making important choices that affect our own lives, we think long and hard and make careful, reasoned decisions—even if those decisions are ultimately subjective ones. We should be just as thorough and just as calculating when making decisions that impact the lives of people in need.

But Wait ... Does That Mean
All Theaters Are Doomed?

Earlier, we saw that the Seva Foundation is far more successful at making the world a better place than the Theatre Communications Group. In general, arts organizations are usually far less successful at achieving the goal of charity than some other types of non-profits. Does this mean that, if we want to be great at doing good, we can never support the arts? If everyone took the approach advocated here, wouldn't it mean that all theaters, operas, ballets, and the like would be doomed to shutter their doors forever?

Certainly not. This is a book about a very specific thing: charity. It is a book about the particular slice of our lives that we devote to doing good, to helping the less fortunate, to making the world a better place.

Most Americans spend a relatively small amount of their time and money on the slice of our lives that we call charity. The average American donates just 3 percent of his or her income to charity each year. The remaining 97 percent is spent on personal needs, wants, goals, and enjoyments.

Similarly, the average American spends just fifteen hours a year volunteering. That's about the equivalent of one full day's worth of waking hours. So the typical person devotes one day each year to carrying out charity, and 364 days to pursuing personal needs, wants, goals, and enjoyments.

It would be wonderful if Americans donated a much larger percentage of their income to charity and volunteered more hours each year. In fact, I recommend it! But right now, for average Americans, the slice of their lives that represents charitable work is a very small one.

What I am proposing is that, in the small sliver of our lives that we call charity—in that small bit of money and time that we set aside to try to make the world a better place—we try to succeed as much as possible at achieving the goal of charity. That is, we put our charitable money and time into the things that will do the most to make the world a better place. We support the causes, organizations, and programs that will alleviate the most suffering and do the most to improve the well-being of others. After all, that is the goal of charity. So if we want to succeed at doing good, that is what we should do. If charity's worth doing, it's worth doing right.

If we took that approach, would it mean that theaters, orchestras, ballets, and any other entity that isn't extremely effective at improving the world would cease to exist? Of course not. The average American would still have 97 percent of his or her money and 364 days a year to put toward whatever he or she wanted, and that includes the arts. Even if you or I were to increase our charitable giving to ten times the national average, we'd still have 70 percent of our income left to spend on theaters, orchestras, and whatever else we wanted.

I give money to lots of things that don't dramatically improve the world: the LA Fitness chain of gyms, my cell phone company, the clothing store H&M, presents for my family at Christmas, and so on. The theaters, orchestras, and ballets of the world have just as much of a place in our society as any of those other things we spend money on, maybe even more of a place. But we should not consider giving money to them to be an efficient act of charity. We should never let our support for such non-profits reduce the amount of time and money we donate to effective ones.

Imagine I give $5,000 a year to charity, with $3,000 of it going to very effective charities like Seva and $2,000 of it going to the Theatre Communications Group. If I want to succeed at charity—that is, if I want to improve the world as much as possible with the slice of my life I devote to charitable giving—I'd give all $5,000 to very effective charities like Seva. If, after that, I still want to support the theater in some way, of course I'm free to do so. But I would consider it a mainly personal pursuit—a pursuit that is fine to have, and that I can enjoy doing, but that isn't efficient charity.

The point is that it's fine to pursue personal goals and to put money toward things that don't dramatically improve the world. None of us is or needs to be a perfectly altruistic creature every second of our lives. But in that slice of life where we do charity work, we should make it count. We should strive to succeed as much as possible. We can do so by supporting the organizations and programs that do the most to make the world a better place.

4

CHASING THE BOTTOM LINE

How to Do More Good for Less Money

Defining Our Bottom Line

In 1985 brothers John, Randy, and Dave Fry, along with John's former girlfriend Kathryn Kolder, opened the first Fry's Electronics store in Sunnyvale, California. The Fry brothers weren't the first in the family to enter the retail market. Their father Charles and uncle Donald were the founders of Fry's Food and Drug Store, a successful supermarket chain that now boasts over one hundred locations around the country. In fact, the seed money that launched Fry's Electronics came from the profits the elder Frys made when they sold their grocery chain to new owners in 1972.

John, Randy, Dave, and Kathryn weren't interested in going into the supermarket business. But they were keenly interested in getting a foothold in the burgeoning 1980s electronics market, and there was no better place to do it than Sunnyvale, which sits just a few miles from the heart of Silicon Valley. So the team set up shop in a 20,000-square-foot space and began stocking the shelves with computers, computer components, circuits, software, microprocessors, and other electronic goods—not to mention t-shirts, books, magazines, and, yes, even some groceries and produce. (The grocery section didn't last long. Advertising promoting the store as a one-stop shop for both computer chips and potato chips failed to win over customers.)

Once the store was up and running, a lot of strategic retail and marketing decisions had to be made—and still have to be made to this day. While the products and parts have changed over the years, the general questions have not.

Should Fry's continue selling off-the-shelf computer components like circuit breakers and microprocessors, or should it replace those with more populist offerings? Should laptop cases or tablet cases be featured in the key end cap spaces near the computer section? How many aisles should be devoted to video games? Should the new flat-screen TVs be retailed at $399 or $449? Is it worth taking out advertising on television and the radio?

For Fry's, as is the case for any other retail outlet, a lot of questions need to be asked and answered on an ongoing basis if they want to be as profitable as possible. It may take testing and slogging through aggregate sales data to find the answers, but the answers will be there. Make no mistake about it, there are right and wrong answers. Certain approaches are better, and certain approaches are worse.

For Fry's, as is the case for any other retail outlet, the determination of which approaches are better and which approaches are worse hinges on one central question: Which approach will make them the most money? If charging $449 for a particular flat-screen TV generates more net revenue than charging $399 for that TV, then charging $449 is the way to go if Fry's wants to be as profitable as possible. If radio advertisements cost more than they generate in increased net revenue, then they probably aren't worth doing.

The bottom line for Fry's and any other business is very simple: it's dollars and cents. If a certain approach will make them more money, they'll do it. If another approach will make them less money, they won't do it. It's easy to measure how successful a business decision is; all they have to do is look at how much money was made or lost. It's also very easy to tell how successful the business is overall; all they have to do is look at how much money it's making. The more money it's making, the more successful it is as a business.

As store owners, John, Randy, Dave, and Kathryn might have other personal goals on top of just making money. They could choose to close their stores on Sunday so that their employees could spend more time with their families. They could decide they don't want to sell products from companies that use sweatshop labor and yank any such products off the shelf, even if it meant a slight dip in revenue. They could decide they want to give their employees a better life, and therefore pay above-industry wages or provide health care packages that were more comprehensive than necessary.

Policies like these would simply indicate that Kathryn and the Fry brothers had other goals in addition to making money. Most business owners do. When it comes to measuring the financial success of the company though, the bottom line remains as clear as ever: How much money is Fry's making? The more money it makes, the more financially successful the company has been.

Just as for-profit businesses have a clear, measurable goal of making money, charity has a clear goal as well: to make the world a better place. In the last two chapters we looked at how, if we really want to succeed, the goal of charity isn't just to "do good." The goal of charity is to do the most good that we can. The goal is to improve the world as much as possible. The more that we reduce the suffering and improve the well-being of others, the more successful we have been at doing charity.

With the help of the genie in the bottle, we were able to estimate how well two charities did at making the world a better place relative to one another. That's very useful information if you're trying to decide where to donate or where to volunteer your time. But what if you're a program manager at Seva? Realizing that your organization does a lot more to improve the world than some other charity might make you feel a slight twinge of pride. But those numbers don't tell you anything about how you, or Seva as an organization, can be more successful. So what *can* tell you that?

To answer, let's step back for a minute and note that, while the ultimate goal of every charitable effort is to make the world a better place, each non-profit has its own specific approach and its own specific goals that tie back to the ultimate aim. A non-profit working to provide clean drinking water to the rural poor has the goal of providing such water to as many people as possible. A non-profit working to fight climate change has the goal of reducing greenhouse gas emissions by as many tons as possible. Some organizations might have multiple goals. For example, an LGBT advocacy organization might be working to achieve marriage equality for as many couples as possible and also to prevent as many LGBT teens as possible from being harassed.

While all charity work has the same ultimate goal of improving the world as much as possible, the specific goal that each non-profit has might be considered its own personal "bottom line." For the rest of the book, we'll use the term "bottom line" to refer to a charity's specific goal. For example, we'll say that clean water charities have a bottom line of providing clean water to people. Hunger relief organizations have a bottom line of preventing people from going hungry.

Just as Fry's can count the dollars on its balance sheet to see how well it's done, individual non-profits can look to their own bottom lines to determine how successful they've been at achieving their goals. The bigger bottom line numbers a non-profit posts, the more successful it has been. If an organization that gives warm, clean clothes to the homeless provided 5,000 people with clothing per year, it might be happy with its work. If it provided 7,000 people with clothing per year, it would probably be even happier. The more needy people the organization helped by providing comfortable clothes, the more successful the organization has been.

And that brings us back to the Seva Foundation and what you as a program manager can do to make Seva even more successful. If you're running Seva, your bottom line is pretty clear: you want to prevent or cure blindness in as many people as you can. If you want to boost your bottom line, and spare even more people from blindness this year than you did last year, you basically have two ways to do that.

First, you can raise more money to put toward your programs. Obviously this is incredibly important. The more money you raise, the more cataract surgeries you can fund. The second way you can spare more people from blindness is by becoming more efficient. That is, you can figure out how to lower the total cost of preventing or curing someone of blindness. For example, if you could devise a way to lower the cost of each cataract surgery by 20 percent, you'd be able to treat a lot more blind people each year—even if your budget didn't go up a dime.

In previous chapters, we said that a particular charity succeeds to the extent it improves the world. Great charities improve the world a whole lot. Mediocre charities improve the world only a moderate amount. Bad charities improve the world only a tiny bit, or make things even worse. While this is true, there is a second and slightly more nuanced way to look at how savvy a particular charity is: namely, to look at how efficient it is. Efficiency is all about doing more with less. In the world of charity, this means doing more good at a lower cost per good done.

If you are a non-profit staffer, efficiency matters *a lot*. If you're more efficient, you can boost your bottom line and do more good for the world. When Seva becomes more efficient, it is able to spare more people from blindness for the same amount of money. When an organization dedicated to clothing the homeless becomes more efficient, it is able to provide clothes to more people in need without spending a penny more.

For an example of how powerful improving efficiency can be, we turn now to a small rabbit rescue in Kalamazoo, Michigan, run by someone very special: you!

Doubling Down on Saving Rabbits

Imagine that you run the Kalamazoo Rabbit Rescue Alliance, an all-volunteer organization whose goal is to take in abandoned, abused, and unwanted rabbits, foster them as long as needed, and then adopt them out to new homes. You started the organization yourself because you love rabbits. You want to save as many of them as you can from being euthanized in the city shelter or from being abandoned by their owners and left to fend for themselves.

You put your heart and soul into your work, and because your organization is a small, volunteer-run outfit, you try to keep costs down as much as possible. About a year into your work, you crunch a few numbers and figure out that it costs you about $100 for each rabbit that you successfully rescue. Just $100 for each rabbit you spare—you're pretty pleased with how well you're doing!

One evening, you sit down for a dinner meeting with another rabbit rescuer from the nearby town of Portage. She runs a group called the Portage Bunny Rescue, which does basically the same work as you do, just in a different town. As you begin to swap stories about your work, she tells you that her group has a particularly streamlined approach for rescuing rabbits. They've lined up volunteer veterinarians who spay and neuter the rabbits free of charge. A local pet store donates rabbit food. Last, they've learned ways to adopt rabbits out more quickly than they had in the past.

With their streamlined approach, it only costs the Portage Bunny Rescue $50 for each rabbit they successfully rescue. Given that you're spending $100 per rabbit spared, you realize that—all other things being equal—your colleague's group is about twice as efficient as yours is at helping rabbits.

At first, after hearing this you're hit with pangs of jealousy and self-doubt. What are you doing wrong? How is it even possible to rescue and re-home a rabbit for just $50? Are there other factors that aren't being considered? But after a little while, your mind snaps back to the whole reason you're running the Kalamazoo Rabbit Rescue Alliance in the first place: you want to save rabbits. So you start asking your colleague questions. You want to learn everything you can from her about exactly what she did to streamline her operations so that you can do the same with yours.

In the months that follow, you do everything you can to cut costs. You call local veterinarians and ask them to donate their time to spay and neuter rabbits. You line up free rabbit food dona-tions from a nearby pet store. You carry out more aggressive and effective adoption campaigns. Over the course of the next year, the plan works; the amount of money you spend for each rabbit you rescue drops from $100 to $85 to $75 to $60. You never quite make it all the way down to $50 per rabbit spared, but you've done a fantastic job.

Thanks to your lowered cost per rabbit rescued, you are now able to save several hundred more rabbits this year than you did last year—despite the fact that the stagnant economy kept your group's budget from growing. Congratulations! After giving yourself a much-deserved pat on the back, let's take a minute to analyze exactly why you succeeded.

First, you defined your bottom line. It was to spare as many rab-bits as possible from being euthanized due to lack of a good home.

Second, you put a price tag on your bottom line. This was your cost per rabbit spared. You realized that, in order to save as many rabbits as possible, you had to drive down your cost per rabbit spared as much as possible.

Third, you made decisions based around your bottom line. You spent time meeting with the Portage Bunny Rescue director to learn from her how to streamline your operations. You changed how you carried out adoptions. You spent time soliciting help from veterinarians and free rabbit food. You did each of these things in order to drive down your cost per rabbit spared. As that cost went down, you were able to rescue hundreds of additional rabbits.

Congratulations on following your bottom line and saving more rabbits—they (and we) thank you!

Where Following the Bottom Line Leads, and Why It Can Be Hard to Follow

All of this sounds probably sounds pretty straightforward. Of course someone rescuing rabbits should try to be as efficient as possible in order to save more rabbits. Don't all non-profits operate that way? Aren't they used to scrimping and saving and doing more with less money?

It would be wonderful if all non-profits acted like you did, defining a bottom line and then doing anything they could to lower their "cost per good done" (cost per HIV infection prevented, cost per ton of greenhouse gas emissions prevented, cost per homeless people clothed, etc.). But the unfortunate reality is that most charitable groups fail to even define a bottom line, let alone make decisions around one. A study by the Center for Effective Philanthropy found that, even among the largest foundations, those with a budget of $100 million or more, only 8 percent had any data whatsoever that showed how successful they'd been at achieving a defined goal. Without that bottom line to guide their decisions, non-profits aren't just shooting in the dark—they don't even know what they're aiming at (*Charity Navigator*, 2010).

Imagine if Fry's Electronics never bothered to track whether their various decisions made them money or lost them money. Did advertising on television and on the radio bring them new business? They wouldn't know. Do circuit boards sell well, or are they a waste of shelf space? They'd have no clue. Even beyond that, if Fry's were operating the same way that 92 percent of major foundations do, they couldn't even tell you how much money they made or lost each year. They wouldn't know whether they were turning a massive profit or sinking deeply into debt. It's possible they could be lucky and end up turning a profit, but with a devil-may-care approach like this, Fry's would almost certainly be bankrupt before long.

It's easy to see how disastrous the results would be if a business failed to define and make decisions around a bottom line. Why is it then that most non-profits fail to do so?

For you and the Kalamazoo Rabbit Rescue Alliance, making the changes you needed to lower your cost per rabbit spared was pretty easy. You didn't have to make any major shifts in how you were doing your work. But for many real-life non-profits, following the bottom line is much like following the yellow brick road in the *Wizard of Oz*. It ends in a pretty amazing place, but getting there is a journey. It may require you to go way outside your comfort zone, to face some things that aren't very easy to face, and to have the courage and self-discipline to stay on the path and keep moving forward toward your end goal.

For an example of how following the bottom line can be a challenge, consider Habitat for Humanity, one of America's most popular charities. Founded in 1976 as a Christian housing ministry, Habitat for Humanity and its volunteers construct simple, affordable new homes and sell them at cost to low-income families who are having trouble affording decent housing on their own. While many people have the perception that Habitat gives homes to very poor or homeless families, they actually don't. Only families that can show they will be able to pay for the house are accepted, and financial audits and credit checks are often run on applicants. Furthermore, although it's more well-known for the new homes it builds, Habitat also devotes a significant portion of its time and resources to rehabilitating existing homes.

Since its founding, Habitat has helped provide more than 750,000 families with decent living conditions through its repairs and new home construction. Along the way it's picked up its share of celebrity support, perhaps none so visible as former President Jimmy Carter, who has actively and publicly volunteered with Habitat for over three decades.

The Habitat family is actually made up of hundreds of individual free-standing non-profits around the world: Habitat for Humanity of Greater Nashville, Dallas Habitat for Humanity, and so forth. Pooled together, these Habitat affiliates rake in a grand total of roughly $1.5 billion a year in donations, which would make Habitat for Humanity one of the fifteen largest charities in America if these were all one organization. The largest chunk of money Habitat receives goes to the original non-profit, whose official name is Habitat for Humanity International. Let's take a look now at Habitat for Humanity International, and to what extent it is following the bottom line in carrying out its charity work.

Just what is the bottom line for Habitat for Humanity? While there may be some secondary goals, the main bottom line is pretty clear: to provide decent housing to as many people as possible. Ask any Habitat staffer or volunteer and that's probably what he or she will tell you. Take a glance at their mission statement and that's what you'll read.

Habitat has done a good job of bringing in more money to put toward its programs. Its revenue has generally increased year over year for the past few decades, topping $300 million in 2013. Because it's been able to bring in more money, it's been able to increase the number of people it provides decent housing to. That's great!

But let's consider efficiency now, as increasing efficiency is the second way that Habitat can increase the number of people it's able to provide decent housing to. In improving efficiency at the Kalamazoo Rabbit Rescue Alliance, you realized that the key figure for you was your cost per rabbit spared. By driving down your cost per rabbit spared, you would be able to rescue many more rabbits each year. What is the key "cost per" for Habitat? It would probably be the cost per family housed, which could happen both through new homes being built or through existing homes being rehabilitated.

Is it possible for Habitat to reduce its cost per family housed? Habitat already works to do that in a number of ways, for example, by using volunteer labor to help carry out the construction work and through finding free or reduced-cost building supplies. But there's another area where Habitat has the opportunity to reduce their cost per family housed even further: it could carry out a larger share of its construction in developing countries.

In their 2013 Annual Report, Habitat for Humanity International notes that, although 70 percent of their program expenses are spent here in the United States, they actually build a larger number of homes in developing countries. How is it that

Habitat could spend less money overseas, and yet still be building more homes there? Because it's much cheaper—perhaps even ten times cheaper—to build a new home in a country like Ghana than it is to build a new home in the United States. Repairs of existing houses are also much cheaper overseas.

Habitat's cost per family housed is much lower in developing countries than it is in the United States. That means that there's a very easy way for Habitat to lower its overall cost per family housed. All it has to do is decrease the number of construction projects it carries out in the United States and increase the number of construction projects overseas. If Habitat did that, its cost per family housed would drop dramatically. The result would be that Habitat would be able to provide far, far more people with decent housing. In fact, it could probably double, possibly even triple, the number of people it's providing with decent housing—all without spending one penny more on programs.

We should note that it might not be wise for Habitat to shift all of its construction work overseas. It has to be conscious of the impact this sort of shift might have on its donors and, therefore, on the amount of funding it receives. Since many of Habitat's donors are American, and since people are more apt to donate toward issues that are close to home, it's possible that if Habitat shifted all of its construction overseas, the amount of money it takes in each year might drop. (On the other hand, it's at least possible that focusing overseas might increase the amount of donations the organization receives, since Habitat could promote the fact that it is helping more families than ever.)

So how much of its construction should Habitat shift overseas if it wants to be able to house as many families as possible? Figuring out the answer is actually pretty easy.

Think back to Fry's Electronics and the question of whether to sell a particular flat-screen TV for $449 or $399. Fry's goal is to make as much money as possible off the sale of these TVs. If Fry's sells the TVs at $449, the company will make more of a profit on each individual set it sells. The only problem is that fewer customers will buy the TV because it's priced a bit higher. What Fry's has to figure out is which price tag is ultimately best for its bottom line. Which price tag ends up generating the most revenue?

To find out, the store might start with its flat-screen TV priced at $399 and then try raising the price to $449. If Fry's makes more of a total profit when the price is $449, the store might then raise the price even higher, to $469. If Fry's makes a still higher total profit at that price, it might raise the price to $489. If profits then began to dip slightly, Fry's would probably go back to $469 and make that the final, ongoing price of the TV. With a bit of tinkering, Fry's would be able to figure out how it could make the most money off sales of its TV.

This is the same sort of question Habitat for Humanity International would answer in trying to balance the fact that overseas construction has a dramatically lower "cost per family housed" with the fact that donors might reduce their giving as a higher and higher percentage of Habitat's work is shifted abroad. Like Fry's, all Habitat would need to do is shift more and more construction overseas until the number of families the organization was able to house began to drop.

To show what this might look like, let's say that next year Habitat increased the amount it spends overseas from 30 percent to 50 percent. At the end of the year, Habitat could count up how many families it had successfully housed compared to the previous year. If Habitat was able to house more families this year (relative to how many families it would have housed had it not made the shift), then the shift worked! This is true even if the amount of donations they receive leveled off or decreased as a result of the shift. The next year Habitat could bump overseas spending up to 60 percent, and the year after that 70 percent. When the number of families it is able to house per year stops going up because of how big the drop in donations has become, that is the point at which Habitat should stop increasing the percentage of money it sends overseas.

One of the implications this would have for Habitat is the following: in order for the organization to be able to house as many people as possible each year, it may need to be willing to let its income go down. For example, imagine that switching from doing 30 percent of construction abroad to doing 90 percent of construction abroad caused Habitat's funding to drop from $300 million to $250 million. That would be a very steep drop! Despite the drop in income though, the total number of families Habitat was able to house that year jumped from 25,000 to a whopping 60,000. Even though its revenue went down, Habitat was able to house many more families because the cost per family housed overseas is so cheap compared to the cost per family housed here in the United States. In other words, Habitat would have been more successful even though its income had gone down.

Habitat for Humanity's bottom line is very clear: to provide decent housing for as many people as possible. If Habitat followed that bottom line, and made all of its decisions around it—like the decision to spend a far higher percentage of its program funds in developing countries—it would be able to significantly boost its bottom-line numbers. It would be able to provide decent housing to far more people than it had before.

Do you think it's likely that Habitat will shift the vast majority of its construction work overseas? Do you think the organization and its executives would be willing to do it, and stick with it, even if it meant the amount of donations it received might go down?

There's no way we can know for sure, but it seems unlikely. For one thing, both individuals and institutions are always very loath to change, so there would be a lot of inertia to overcome. Second, Habitat's employees and directors likely have the same psychological biases that all of us have: to focus more on those who are closer to us and similar to us, in this case Americans. (We'll talk more about that phenomenon in a later chapter.) Third, it is a very rare charity that would be willing to let the amount of money it takes in drop if that's what needs to happen for it to be able to accomplish more good. While there are no practical barriers preventing Habitat from shifting most of its work overseas, the psychological barriers will probably prevent the organization from ever doing so.

Forget what Habitat may or may not do in the future though. The very fact that the organization has not already made this switch illustrates the fact that even highly professional and highly respected charities often fail to base key decisions around their bottom line. This is not unique to Habitat for Humanity. Habitat is not being singled out here because it does a particularly poor job of following the bottom line. Habitat does important work, and it's great that they put at least a portion of their money into overseas building. We are just spotlighting Habitat to give one easy-to-explain example of a phenomenon that exists across the entire charity field. Non-profits both large and small often fail to define and make decisions around a clear bottom line.

When Following the Bottom Line Means Making Big Changes

While it seems unlikely that Habitat for Humanity International will ever spend the vast majority of its program funds overseas—especially if doing so caused its revenue to go down—it's at least possible. Habitat already spends 30 percent of its program funds overseas, so it's conceivable that figure could shift to 50 percent, 60 percent, or even 70 percent in the coming years. It would represent a shift in how Habitat prioritizes different geographic areas, but it wouldn't be breaking new ground for them. In fact, it would be pretty much business as usual, just with more business in one part of the world and less business in another.

Following the bottom line can sometimes require making much more dramatic changes. When it does, the psychological barriers that need to be overcome can be even more imposing. Consider for example the Make-A-Wish Foundation.

In the spring of 1980, Arizona-based U.S. Customs Agent Tommy Austin had a problem. His wife's friend had a seven-year-old son, Chris Greicius, who was dying of leukemia. Chris's dream had been to be a police officer, so Austin wanted to arrange some sort of special police-style experience for Chris before he died. Unfortunately, the Customs office was not being very accommodating. There seemed to be miles of red tape standing in the way of doing something good for Chris before he died.

Then, on a stakeout near the Mexico border, Austin befriended an officer from the Arizona Department of Public Safety. One story and one phone call later, the DPS officially agreed to team up with Austin to provide Chris the experience of a lifetime.

On the big day, a DPS helicopter picked Chris up from the Scottsdale Memorial Hospital where he was being treated. Chris was flown to the nearby Department of Public Safety headquarters, where he was given a tour and issued his own hat and badge as an honorary officer. Some DPS employees, warmed by meeting the smiling seven-year-old, spent that night putting together a custom-tailored police uniform for Chris, which they presented to him the following day.

Chris died not long after, but word of his special experience began to spread. Department of Public Safety officers and their wives began talking about setting up a foundation to help more sick children live out their dreams before they died. That summer a small group of officers, along with their families and friends, launched what would soon become the Make-A-Wish Foundation.

To this day, Make-A-Wish has continued to carry out its signature activity with children who are suffering from life-threatening diseases: providing a one-time "wish experience," such as a meeting a ballerina, flying in a helicopter, or being a superhero. The wish experience may last an hour, a day, or several days, although it is a one-time event.

Make-A-Wish has grown by leaps and bounds from its humble beginnings in the early 1980s. Most Americans are familiar with the organization and what it does, and its catchy approach has been woven into the plot lines of numerous TV shows. As of 2013, the annual income for the Foundation (including both the national group and all of its local affiliates) was a staggering $264 million. That year, 14,003 wishes were granted to children in need.

What is the Make-A-Wish Foundation's bottom line? Make-A-Wish's signature activity and its claim to fame is a very specific type of activity: granting sick and dying children a wonderful wish experience. So it might seem like the bottom line of Make-A-Wish is to grant wishes, and that what the Foundation could do to improve is to increase the number of wishes it grants.

But providing a wish experience is not an end in itself. It is a *tool*. It is a tool that Make-A-Wish uses to bring about its actual bottom-line goal: to make suffering children happier. That's certainly an admirable bottom line! And the greater the number of suffering children Make-A-Wish makes happier, the more successful the organization would be.

Before we dive further into the Make-A-Wish Foundation and its bottom line, let's turn for a moment to another charity that also has the goal of making suffering children happier: the Schistosomiasis Control Initiative. That big, hard-to-pronounce word is the name of a tropical disease found in Africa, Asia, and South America. Schistosomiasis is spread by parasitic worms that enter the bodies of people bathing, swimming, or wading in infected areas.

Although it is not usually lethal, the disease affects about 200 million people worldwide each year. Symptoms can include diarrhea, bloody stools or urine, abdominal pain, fever, fatigue, and skin lesions. In children it is also known to cause poor growth, learning difficulty, and malnutrition. Perhaps worst of all, schistosomiasis is a chronic disease. In those who have been infected, liver damage, kidney failure, and bladder cancer can occur. About twenty million people suffer from debilitating cases of the disease, many of them children.

The good news is that schistosomiasis can be quickly and effectively treated with a single dose of deworming medicine.

SCI works to provide this treatment to as many people as possible, with particular emphasis on children. Moreover, the work is cheap. SCI spends less than $1 for each child it deworms, and less than $1,000 for each child it spares from a lifetime of debilitating disease.

The results that SCI brings about are similar to those that the Make-A-Wish Foundation brings about. The goal of both organizations is to improve the lives of sick children. One difference is that the wish experience the Make-A-Wish Foundation provides lasts just a few hours or a day. It may add to the child's happiness for a few days or weeks beforehand and afterward, but the impact basically ends there. SCI's work, on the other hand, lasts much longer. For all of the children it treats, it ends the bout of sickness that child is going through. For some of the children it treats, SCI prevents an entire lifetime's worth of debilitating chronic disease.

Another difference between the two organizations is the cost per suffering child made happier. SCI's "cost per" is $1 per suffering child it makes happier for the few weeks or months that child would have experienced the symptoms of schistosomiasis. And the "cost per" is $1,000 for each child who is spared from a lifetime of debilitating disease. Based on the Make-A-Wish Foundation's revenue and number of wishes granted in 2013, its "cost per" appears to be about $19,000 per sick child made temporarily much happier.

As was the case with the Seva Foundation and the Theatre Communications Group, we can see there's a big difference in impact between SCI and the Make-A-Wish Foundation. For one thing, SCI's cost per sick child made happier is dramatically lower. On top of that, for many of the children it treats, SCI has a major lifelong impact, freeing them from a lifetime of debilitating disease. The Make-A-Wish Foundation's impact only lasts for a very short period of time.

Imagine now that the heads of the Make-A-Wish Foundation have just gone over these figures. What kind of reaction do you think they would have? What do you think they would do?

If the Make-A-Wish Foundation wants to succeed as much as possible at its bottom-line goal—if it wants to help the largest number of sick kids possible, and have the biggest impact on them—it would do well to switch a portion of its budget over to funding the work that the Schistosomiasis Control Initiative is doing. (Or to funding the work that some other similarly high-impact children's health charity is doing.) By doing so, Make-A-Wish would dramatically lower its cost per suffering child made happier. That means Make-A-Wish would be able to make a much larger number of sick kids happier each year, and also have a much longer-lasting impact on them.

Consider, for example, what would happen if Make-A-Wish established a new program called "Wish To Be Well." The goal of this program would be to grant children in Africa their "wish to be well" by providing those who are infected with schistosomiasis with medicine so that they don't develop a lifelong debilitating disease. Make-A-Wish decided that it would spend 10 percent of its total budget on this new program.

Last year, Make-A-Wish's total accomplishment for sick children was granting 14,000 of them a wish experience. This year, with 10 percent of their budget going to the new Wish To Be Well program, Make-A-Wish's total accomplishment for sick children for the year would be the following: granting 12,600 of them a wish experience; sparing 26,400 of them from a lifetime of debilitating disease; and sparing 26 million of them from the pains of a bout of schistosomiasis.

Which of these two outcomes is better for sick children? Which of these two approaches is more successful at achieving the goal of charity, namely reducing suffering and increasing well-being?

Further, if Make-A-Wish devoted just 10 percent of its budget to a program like this, it's almost certain that donors would not bat an eye. The amount of revenue the organization takes in would not be affected. Make-A-Wish could continue to focus the majority of its promotional materials and funding appeals around wish granting, while making only occasional mention of the new program.

And that's just what Make-A-Wish could accomplish by putting 10 percent of its budget toward more efficient work. If they upped that figure to 25 percent, they could still grant 10,500 sick children their wishes, down only slightly from the original number of 14,000. But Make-A-Wish would also now spare 66,000 children from a lifetime of debilitating disease and protect 66 million more from the pains of a schistosomiasis infection. If they spent 50 percent of their budget on this work, they could wipe out 130 million cases of schistosomiasis and spare 132,000 children from a lifetime of crippling disease—all while still providing thousands of wish experiences each year.

If Make-A-Wish wants to improve the lives of sick children as much as possible, it would do well to keep increasing the percentage of its budget it spends on more efficient work until the number of sick kids it is able to help each year stops growing. As was the case in the Habitat for Humanity example, taking this approach would require Make-A-Wish to be open to the possibility that it could experience a decrease in total yearly revenue. (Make-A-Wish's funding could go down if the public is less interested in funding children's health initiatives in Africa than they are with granting wishes for dying children in America—which is probably the case.)

While a significant shift in program funding like this may have to be rolled out slowly, and in some cases may even require slight modifications to a non-profit's mission statement and charter, in practical terms it is very doable. It's also been done before, including by some of the country's biggest charities.

For nearly a century the main focus of the YMCA was to provide safe housing in a Christian environment for young men and women who had moved from rural areas to big cities in order to find jobs.

Today the organization is focused mainly on inspiring children and their families to exercise and be healthy. Despite that dramatic change in focus, the Y has continued to prosper. As of 2013 it was the second largest charity in the country in terms of total revenue, and among the ten largest in terms of private support.

Similarly, in its first few decades the American Cancer Society focused primarily on educating the public about cancer in an attempt to de-stigmatize the disease and to increase the public's interest in finding treatments and cures. Today the ACS focuses more on patient support, medical research, and testing, with only a small fraction of its budget going to increase public awareness about the disease. While its central focus of combating cancer has remained, the type of work it does to combat the disease has changed significantly over time. These shifts certainly haven't interfered with the organization's growth: the American Cancer Society now takes in nearly a billion dollars a year in revenue.

Do you think the Make-A-Wish Foundation will ever shift a small portion of its budget away from providing wish experiences and toward another type of work that does far more good for sick children? Again, while there's no way for us to predict the future, it seems unlikely that Make-A-Wish will ever do this. For one thing, Make-A-Wish and its directors would face all of the same psychological barriers we mentioned earlier when discussing Habitat for Humanity: individual and organizational inertia; the innate bias we all have toward helping those closer to us (Americans); and a reluctance to do anything that might reduce the amount of funding the organization takes in.

On top of that, Make-A-Wish directors would have another, perhaps even bigger, psychological barrier to overcome before they could make the shift. They would need to overcome the strong desire we all have for *consistency* and for having a *consistent identity*.

The Make-A-Wish Foundation has been doing one thing and one thing only since it was started nearly twenty-five years ago: granting wishes for sick and dying children. The idea that it should spend even a portion of its money on something other than granting kids their wishes might sound laughable, and perhaps even a bit naïve.

"Of *course* Make-A-Wish is going to keep focusing all of its programs on granting wishes," we can imagine one of the Foundation's directors saying. "That is what we were created to do. It's who we are. It's what we do. We are not a schistosomiasis organization. It's great that other organizations are working on that issue, but it's not our issue. It's just not what we do."

That certainly sounds logical. But if we think more critically about it, we'll realize that however logical it may sound or may be, at the end of the day the following still remains unavoidably true: sick children will be much, much better off if Make-A-Wish puts a percentage of its budget toward more efficient programs like fighting schistosomiasis.

If Make-A-Wish does put money toward that, then tens of thousands of children, children with a name and a smile and a family and a favorite color, will be spared from an entire lifetime of debilitating disease. Only a very small number of children will miss out on a temporary wish experience. If Make-A-Wish does not put money toward that, those tens of thousands of children are going to be condemned to a lifetime of debilitation. In fact that is exactly what happened last year, and the year before that, and the year before that, because Make-A-Wish made the choice to prioritize granting wishes over other, more efficient ways of making sick children happier.

All of the logic, reasoning, and arguments we may have for why *not* to shift toward more efficient programs will always be overshadowed by the stark reality of what will happen if we don't. If in spite of the outcome we still think Make-A-Wish should focus just on granting wishes, it suggests that we may be prioritizing consistency and consistency of identity over the lives of those children. It suggests that it's more important to us that an organization stays "what it's supposed to be," and what it's always been, than that as many sick children as possible are helped.

If we want to be great at doing good, if we want to make the world as much of a better place as possible, we need to remain focused on the bottom-line outcomes. Exactly how much good are we accomplishing? How many sick kids are we helping? How many needy families are we providing homes for? And most importantly, what changes could we make—even major changes—that would allow us to help even more of them?

Asking those questions, and having the discipline and courage to make changes based on the answers, can be challenging. But it will enable us to make the world a far, far better place.

Why We Lose Sight of the Bottom Line

In theory, it seems like following the bottom line should come naturally to us. After all, the whole reason we donate or volunteer or carry out non-profit work is because we want to help children, feed the hungry, protect victims of abuse, and so forth. Shouldn't our brains' default mode motivate us to act in a way that helps as many of those who suffer as possible?

And it certainly seems like non-profits themselves should be able to get this right. After all, they are doing this work full time. Plus, for most non-profit staffers, they're not doing the work they do because they take home a big fat paycheck; they're doing it because they truly care about the issue. Shouldn't it be a given that they would put time into determining which approaches will "get more out" and then take those approaches?

There are a number of reasons why so few non-profits base their decisions around a clearly defined bottom line, but let's start with one particularly depressing one: *they don't have to.* Non-profits can ignore the bottom line and still survive and, in fact, can even thrive in terms of how much money they take in from donors. The stunning growth of the Make-A-Wish Foundation is a clear testament to that.

In the for-profit world, taking your eyes off the bottom line is an existential threat. That's because in the for-profit world, taking in revenue and achieving the bottom-line goal are one and the same. If a business wants to continue existing, it can only do so by paying close attention to how much money it's making.

In the non-profit world things are different. For charities, the bottom-line goal of helping sick children, reducing greenhouse gas emissions, and so forth is separate from the process of generating revenue from donors. Sure, the reason people donate to an environmental organization may be because the group is trying to reduce greenhouse gas emissions. But the exact amount of emissions the non-profit prevents from entering the atmosphere doesn't have a big impact on how much money the organization raises. Whether the Sierra Club prevents 100,000 tons or 10,000,000 tons of carbon emissions is not going to have much of an impact on how much money donors give the group. What will have an impact is how skilled its communications and fundraising departments are at inspiring people to give, how emotionally engaging the organization's cause is for the general public, and how well-known the organization is.

Because the bottom-line goal of improving the world is separate from the process of raising money, non-profits aren't forced to focus intently on their bottom-line. They can continue to exist and grow even if their bottom-line results are not particularly great, or could be dramatically better. If donors began to pick which charities to support based on the bottom-line results each organization has, you can be sure this would change very quickly. We'll talk more about that in a later chapter. Right now though, non-profits have little need and little financial incentive to pay close attention to their bottom line.

In addition to the lack of financial incentive, why else do non-profits fail to base decisions around a bottom line?

One major reason is simply a lack of exposure to the idea. Few non-profits take this approach, so most non-profit workers have never learned to think in these terms. It's a way of doing charity that sounds obvious once you hear it, but that may not occur to you on your own—especially when everyone around you is operating in a different way.

Second, as we'll discuss in depth in a later chapter, our brains seem almost hardwired to steer us away from carrying out charity in a logical, efficient manner. The very fact that we don't instinctively take a bottom-line approach suggests that many of our charity decisions may have more to do with satisfying personal needs (such as feeling good for standing up for what we believe in, feeling connected to a cause, or dispelling the upset we feel at injustice) than with creating the best real-world outcomes that we can. This is as true for donors and volunteers as it is for non-profit staffers.

We also have a variety of psychological biases standing in the way of making better charity choices, some of which were touched on earlier. We have a bias toward wanting to help those who are similar to us, such as those who live in the same country or the same city as we do. This can cause us to overlook lower "cost per" opportunities for doing good in other places. Both individuals and organizations tend to want things to stay the same; we have a well-documented bias toward thinking that the current approach to a problem is the best approach. We are also reluctant to acknowledge that we could be doing things better. We'll discuss these and other biases at greater length later in the book.

Third, it's just easier to not take a bottom-line approach. Defining a bottom line and basing decisions around it requires time and mental energy. It adds an additional question to every decision an organization makes: "What impact will this have on our bottom line?" Without an organizational culture that demands such thinking, or an incentive system that rewards it, few people will put in the extra work to always ask and answer that question, even when they care deeply about the cause. All of us have a preference for doing things the easy way, and that carries over into the charity decisions we make, whether as non-profit staffers, donors, or volunteers.

Last, taking a bottom-line approach is counterintuitive. Many people who go into non-profit work do so because they don't want their life's work to be based around dollar signs. The charity world is filled with people who left jobs as accountants, sales reps, marketers, managers, and other profit- and numbers-oriented professions because they wanted to make more of a difference with their lives and get away from bean counting. Plus, most of us who are trying to do good, whether as donors or volunteers, are doing so because we're driven by empathy for the plight of an individual who is in need. That's not the time and place where we're inclined to stop and make dispassionate calculations. So even though a bottom-line approach will help us better succeed at improving the world, taking that approach doesn't come naturally.

All of the above barriers help explain why most non-profits, and most of us as individuals, often fail to base our charity decisions around a clear bottom line. But the fact is that, without a bottom-line approach, our charity work will always fall far short of its potential. As disrupting as it can be to the way we do charity work now, and as loath as we are to realize we could be doing something better, if we want to succeed there is nothing more important than a single-minded focus on the bottom line. Until non-profits choose to adopt such an approach, or are compelled to do so by donors, the people, animals, and ecosystems they are trying to help will always be short-changed. Until we as individuals adopt such an approach, we will also fall short of our potential for doing good.

For those of us who don't work at a non-profit, but who do donate to charitable causes, what would adopting a bottom-line approach look like for us? To find out, let's take a trip back to Kalamazoo, Michigan.

5

WHY EFFICIENCY MEANS EVERYTHING FOR DONORS (AND CHARITIES, TOO)

Bringing It Back to the Bunnies

Imagine that you volunteer once a month with the previously mentioned Kalamazoo Rabbit Rescue Alliance. (Sorry, in this scenario you're not the founder anymore, just a regular old volunteer.) It's not particularly glamorous work—mostly cleaning cages, refilling water bottles, and giving the rabbits some loving attention—but that's fine with you. You just want to do what you can to make life a little better for these rabbits and to help the Alliance run as smoothly as possible.

Before long, you become good friends with the Alliance's founder. You have a lot of respect for her, for the hard work she's put in to creating and running this all-volunteer operation and for saving the lives of so many rabbits. One day you are chatting with her and you wonder just how much money it costs to keep the whole operation going. She tells you that she actually just recently looked over the figures, and it turns out that it costs the Alliance about $100 for each rabbit that it rescues. "Wow," you think to yourself. "Just $100 to save a life!" Your respect for the Alliance and its founder grows even more.

After volunteering there for a number of months, the inevitable happens: you adopt one of the rabbits. It's a large white New Zealand rabbit named Mr. Muffin, who'd been at the shelter for a particularly long amount of time because his advanced age made him less attractive to most adopters.

Mr. Muffin fits right in at your home, happily bouncing around his corner of the house and not doing any of the bad things that rabbits sometimes do like chewing electrical cords or eating the paint off walls. Within weeks he is a cherished part of the family; it's hard to imagine life without him!

A bit later in the year, you invite family, friends, and a few other rabbit rescuers over for a Christmas party at your house. While munching on some appetizers, you start talking shop with a friend of yours who volunteers at the nearby Portage Bunny Rescue. Funding issues come up—small rescues like yours are always stretched thin—and you recall your conversation with the Kalamazoo Rabbit Rescue Alliance's founder. You let your friend know that, while money may be tight, the good news is that for the Alliance it costs only $100 to rescue each of the rabbits they rescue.

"That's great," your friend says, "and actually at Portage, it's even lower. We spend only about $50 for every rabbit we rescue!"

"Wow," you reply. "How is that even possible?"

"It took a lot of work, but it's really paid off. We get free rabbit food donated by a big pet store in our area. There's a veterinarian we know who has agreed to do all of the spay and neuter surgeries on the rabbits for free. We've also learned a couple of very effective tricks for getting rabbits adopted out more quickly to good homes."

You're impressed, but before you can reply another friend steps into the conversation and the topic moves on to other things.

Flash forward a couple of weeks and its December 28. You're sitting at the kitchen table, mug of hot chocolate in your hand, thinking about what year-end charitable donations you want to make. You look over your bank account and decide that you're going to donate $1,000. Since rescuing rabbits is your favorite cause, that is what you're going to donate toward.

You pull out your checkbook and get ready to write a $1,000 check to the Kalamazoo Rabbit Rescue Alliance. You think about the founder and how grateful she'll be for the donation. You also think about all the rabbits in cages at the Alliance "headquarters" (really just the founder's heated garage), waiting desperately for a new home. You hope that your $1,000 will help some of them find that new home.

So you put your pen to the paper, but before you start to fill out the check you recall the conversation you had at your Christmas party with the friend of yours who works at the Portage Bunny Rescue. At Portage, they only spend $50 for each rabbit they rescue. At Kalamazoo, it costs about $100 for each rabbit rescued. Both organizations are strapped for cash. Both would be able to rescue more rabbits if they had more money. So now you start to wonder which rescue you should donate to.

If you donate to the Kalamazoo Rabbit Rescue Alliance, your money will probably help save about ten rabbits. If you give to the Portage Bunny Rescue, you will probably help save about twenty.

"But wait," you think to yourself. "Sure, Portage may have figured out a cheaper way to rescue rabbits, but the Kalamazoo Rabbit Rescue Alliance is like my second home. Those are the rabbits that I'm seeing in cages every month when I go in to volunteer. I know each one of them by name. I know how much they need this money so the Alliance can help find them a good home. Plus, the people who work there are good people, they are friends—and I want to support my friends. To top off, Kalamazoo is my town, and the Alliance is our rabbit rescue. Shouldn't I focus first on the need that exists here in my own community?"

You take a few sips of hot chocolate and mull it over a bit more, and you realize that what you're facing is a conflict of goals. One goal you have is to save as many rabbits as possible from being euthanized or left in abusive situations. Pursuing that goal would mean donating to Portage. But another goal you have is to support a good organization that is near and dear to you on many levels (as well as to support the friends and friendly rabbits you know there). Pursuing that goal would mean donating to Kalamazoo. So what do you do?

It's at times like this that it's worth thinking back to Oskar Schindler and the profound regret he felt at the end of World War II. Far from being filled with pride at the many people he had saved—people he knew, people he was friends with, people whose hands he could shake in the factory each day—he felt regret. Regret for the faceless, nameless (to him) people he could have saved had he only approached his work in a more thoughtful, rigorous manner. Schindler was filled with regret because he knew that he could have "got more out" but had lacked the forethought and self-discipline to do so.

If our goal is charity—making the world a better place, in this case through rescuing rabbits—donating to the Portage Bunny Rescue is clearly the better choice. Rabbits overall will be better off if you donate to Portage. That we happen to live in Kalamazoo instead of neighboring Portage doesn't really matter. That the Kalamazoo Rabbit Rescue Alliance is the organization we happened to start volunteering with, adopting from, and befriending the staff and the bunnies at is a matter of chance. While the Alliance may have great emotional value to us, and while we may identify strongly with it, the fact remains that donating to the Portage Rabbit Rescue will save twice as many rabbits from being killed. If our main priority is making the world a better place, and if our main priority is helping rabbits, then that fact is of far greater importance than anything else.

The Space to Be Human

Looking at a situation from afar, it's often easy to see what the right thing to do is. Of course, Schindler should have sold his car and used the money to save more Jewish individuals from the terror of the concentration camps. Of course, saving the lives of ten additional rabbits is more important than having one person write a check to his local shelter instead of a neighboring one.

In their great book *Decisive*, brothers Chip and Dan Heath (the pair who also wrote *Made to Stick* and *Switch*) share easy-to-use tools that can help us make smarter decisions. One of the key principles the Heath brothers cover is the importance of attaining distance before making a decision. Our short-term emotion often leads us to make choices that aren't ideal. When we can step back and get some perspective, it's usually easier for us to realize what the right decision is (Heath & Heath, 2013).

Considering fictional examples, as we're doing here and as we did with the genie in the bottle scenario, is one way to do that. Another tool that the Heath brothers recommend is to imagine what we'll think ten years from now. Ten years later, do you think we'll look back and wish we had given that one check to the rabbit rescue we volunteered with at the time instead of the rescue in a neighboring town? Probably not. On the other hand, ten years later we may indeed look back, as Schindler did, regretting that we could have "got more out," we could have saved the lives of ten more rabbits, but failed to do so.

But taking a distanced, calculated approach on decisions like these isn't easy. We aren't altruistic robots who can just shut off our emotions and preferences and desires and do perfect good all the time. We all need space—plenty of space—to be human. To go with our gut. To respond from and act from the emotional part of our brain. To do things a certain way because that's just the way we want to do them. To act out of instinctual empathy and kindness because it feels good, and because it feels like that should be a part of who we are and how we live our lives.

We should do all of those things on a regular basis. They are an important part of what it means to be a happy, healthy human being. In our personal relationships, in our friendships, in our hobbies, in our free time, there are limitless opportunities to do what feels good, to do what comes naturally, to support what we happen to like, to act out of the instinctual empathy that bubbles up in us without having to second guess it.

But in the small slice of our lives that represents charity—in the small percentage of our money and our time that we devote to making the world a better place—it is there we should put those personal needs aside and just focus on succeeding as much as possible. Because that slice of life is not about doing what we want; it is about doing what will help others. And because in that small slice of life, *so very much* is on the line with the decisions we make—so many real lives, so much real suffering, so much real happiness.

If I were the volunteer at the Kalamazoo Rabbit Rescue Alliance trying to make my year-end donation decision, I can certainly see myself considering all of the above and being exasperated. I can picture myself thinking, "All right, all right, I get it, but geez … can't I just donate to the group I *want* to donate to, the group I'm volunteering with every month? Is that too much to ask?"

Of course we can donate to the Kalamazoo rescue if we want to. It's our money and it's our choice. But regardless of what is fair, reasonable, our right, or anything else, there is one very simple and very inescapable fact that will still remain inexorably true: if we do donate to Kalamazoo instead of Portage, ten bunnies we could have saved will die.

The choice is indeed ours. But in the slice of our lives where we make charity decisions like these, I hope that our choice will be to do the most good we can.

There Are Massive Differences Between Charities in the Same Field

In the last chapter we looked at how efficiency is key for those who work at non-profits. Driving down the cost per sick child made happier or the cost per family housed is one of the main ways that charities like the Make-A-Wish Foundation and Habitat for Humanity can be more successful and help more people.

But efficiency is also key for donors. In fact, when it comes to deciding where to donate, efficiency is everything. If I'm trying to decide between different charities, the key question I need to ask myself is not, "Which non-profit is improving the world the most?" Instead, the question I need to ask myself is this: "Which non-profit will improve the world the most with my donation?" That is really just another way of asking: Which non-profit accomplishes the most good per dollar spent? Which non-profit is most efficient?

In deciding whether to donate $1,000 to the Kalamazoo Rabbit Rescue Alliance or to the Portage Bunny Rescue, it doesn't really matter how big each organization is. The Kalamazoo Rabbit Rescue Alliance could be a million-dollar organization, and the Portage Bunny Rescue could have an annual budget of a few thousand bucks. Or it could be the other way around. Similarly, the grand total of how many rabbits each group saves each year doesn't really matter. Kalamazoo could save 10,000 rabbits a year and Portage could save 100. Or it could be the other way around. Either way, it doesn't matter.

All that matters to us is the cost per rabbit spared at each organization. Kalamazoo has a $100 cost per rabbit spared, and Portage has a $50 cost per rabbit spared. That single piece of information tells us exactly what we need to know about what we will accomplish if we donate to each group. It tells us that if we donate $1,000 to Kalamazoo we will probably save about ten rabbits, and if we donate to Portage we will probably save about twenty.

Small organizations can be more efficient than large organizations. Because of their low overhead and their need to make every dollar count, they may be able to have a lower "cost per" than similar larger organizations. On the other hand, large organizations can be more efficient than their smaller counterparts. They can leverage their larger platform and expertise to accomplish big things small organizations cannot, which can give them a lower "cost per" than smaller groups. Rather than look to the size of a charity or the total amount of good a charity is doing for the world, the key thing donors should look to is how much good a charity does per dollar spent.

When we compare charities—even very similar charities, like two rabbit rescues—on how much good they accomplish per dollar spent, what we see can be shocking. Earlier, we saw what a massive difference in impact there is between the Seva Foundation and the Theatre Communications Group, two organizations in different charitable fields. When we look around though, we'll see that there aren't just big differences in impact between non-profits in different fields. There are also big differences in impact between charities in the same field. Let's take a look at a fictitious example now before moving on to some real ones.

Imagine that one day Allison, a twenty-two-year-old grad student at Western Michigan University in Kalamazoo, decided she wanted to do something to help rabbits. Like the rabbit rescue directors, she too wanted fewer rabbits languishing in cages and fewer rabbits being killed due to lack of a good home. After doing some online research, she learned there were a couple main problems that led people who had rabbits to abandon them or turn them over to organizations like the Kalamazoo Rabbit Rescue Alliance.

One common problem Allison found was something we referenced earlier: people became frustrated when rabbits chewed on furniture, electrical cables, and other household items. Another common problem was that people didn't know the few basic rules they should be following to keep their rabbits healthy. Rabbits would get sick, and as the veterinary bills mounted people would think that having a rabbit just wasn't worth it, so they would get rid of them.

Once Allison felt she had a pretty good understanding of the main problems that were causing so many rabbits to be abandoned and to therefore need new homes, she came up with a plan to try to prevent some of those problems from occurring. First, over the course of a couple weeks she created RabbitGuide.com, a simple website that explained how to solve common rabbit problems. The site offered an email address and phone number people could call for advice if they were having issues with their rabbits. She also created a short brochure that contained the same information as the website. Allison then reached out to local pet stores, individual breeders who sold rabbits out of their homes, and shelters that adopted out rabbits in the greater Kalamazoo area. After some cajoling, all of them agreed to provide one of her brochures and a flyer about her website to everyone who bought or adopted a rabbit from them.

Since all Allison had to do was set up a website and print some brochures, her work turned out to be pretty cheap. (And that was certainly good, since she was a grad student.) The whole thing cost just $400, plus some time to set things in motion. And guess what: it worked! Thanks to the helpful advice that people now had, the number of rabbits being abandoned to the Kalamazoo Rabbit Rescue Alliance and other local shelters began to drop. In fact, over the course of the year the number of rabbits that were abandoned dropped by 100. Because in Michigan (as in most states) there are always far more rabbits needing homes than there are people willing to adopt, this meant that 100 more rabbits stayed in good homes instead of languishing in cages or being euthanized.

At the end of the year, what was Allison's "cost per rabbit saved"? It was not $100, as it was for the Kalamazoo Rabbit Rescue Alliance, or even $50, as it was for the Portage Bunny Rescue. Allison's cost per rabbit saved was a mere $4—more than ten times lower than either of the local rabbit rescues. One young grad student working alone, with almost no budget and with little experience, was ten times more efficient at saving rabbits than the experienced rabbit rescue organizations that had been operating for years.

While this is a fictional example, it speaks to some surprising realities of non-profit work. For one thing, different charities and different approaches in the same field can be and often are dramatically different in efficiency. One approach can be exponentially more cost-effective than another. Second, the most efficient approach is sometimes one that is neither glamorous nor particularly interesting, nor emotionally gratifying for donors, volunteers, or non-profit workers. It can sometimes come from unlikely sources, and in unlikely forms.

Consider, for example, the real world of animal protection. It's a world I know fairly well, as it's the world I've worked in professionally for the past ten years. It's also a good field to use as an example here because, while the specific work each animal protection charity does may vary, the bottom line is always the same: to protect animals. In some cases that may involve keeping a dog alive and well by finding a home for her when she would otherwise be euthanized. In other cases it may mean preventing an animal from enduring a miserable life and a painful death, for example, by reducing the consumer demand for fur. In still other cases it may mean reducing the cruelty done to animals by bringing about legislative protections for animals, such as banning the practice of confining mother pigs in tiny metal cages on pig farms. Finally, in still other cases, it may involve preventing the destruction of a particular patch of woodlands or rain forest so that the wild animals living there can continue to exist.

All of these approaches lead back to the same bottom line of protecting as many animals as possible. That's a fairly easy bottom line to quantify. The more animals a non-profit has protected, the more successful it has been. Preventing ten pit bulls from being abused by a dog-fighting ring is good. Preventing 100 pit bulls from being abused by a dog-fighting ring is a whole lot better.

Actually, it's not just the number of animals helped that matters. The degree to which those animals have been helped matters as well. We would probably all agree that sparing one person from blindness is a greater good than providing one person with a free back massage. Even though one person is helped in both situations, the degree of help provided in each is drastically different. Similarly, the amount of good an animal protection organization does for each animal matters. Preventing an animal from being smacked in the face one time is good. Preventing an animal from having to endure a lifetime of misery in a cage so small she can barely turn around, as is common on many puppy mills, factory farms, and similar locations, is a whole lot better.

So what would a very successful animal protection organization look like? If we're following the bottom line, a successful animal charity would be one that helps a large number of animals and that provides a very large degree of help to those animals.

Like many of the points brought up in this book, the idea of trying to help as many animals as much as possible seems painfully obvious. We would expect that animal protection groups would work to help as many animals as possible. We would expect they would work to help the types of animals that are most badly abused.

Unfortunately, this is not the approach that most animal protection organizations take. As a result, when we compare different animal protection groups against one another, we see that there are immense differences in how much good each organization does for animals.

Of the roughly 23,000 animal protection, welfare, and services organizations recognized as non-profits by the IRS, almost all of them are animal rescues or animal shelters. The primary tool these organizations use to help animals is to take in animals that would otherwise be euthanized, care for them at a shelter, and in most cases adopt them out to new guardians. Some of them also spay or neuter the animals they work with to reduce the number of animals that will need homes in the future. While most groups focus on cats and dogs, there are also rescues and shelters for horses, birds, amphibians, farmed animals, wild animals, and so forth.

This sort of work is exactly what most members of the public picture when they think of animal protection work: organizations rescuing cats, dogs, or occasionally other animals and finding new homes for them. Donation patterns reflect that as well, as the large majority of money donated to animal charities goes to organizations that do exclusively or primarily rescue and shelter work.

But is rescuing individual animals really the best way to help animals? Thinking about the bottom line, is that the approach that will enable animal charities to help the greatest number of animals and to help them to the greatest degree?

To help find the answer, let's consider the Humane Society of the United States.

In 1954, journalist Fred Myers and several other leaders of local animal protection groups met to discuss the creation of a national humane society. The animal welfare problems that each of their groups was trying to address were national in scope, and Myers felt that having one unifying organization would give the American humane movement the strength it needed to tackle some of those issues. The new organization's home would be Washington, D.C., ground zero for creating national legislative change. That year, the group that would soon be called the Humane Society of the United States (HSUS) was born.

While most people associate the term "humane society" with cat and dog shelters, from the time of its founding HSUS has sought to address all animal protection issues. One of its early successes was helping unite animal protection organizations around the country in support of the Humane Slaughter Act of 1958, which provided some modest welfare protections for cows, pigs, horses, and sheep being killed in slaughterhouses. Since then, HSUS has remained active on a range of animal issues, from supporting local shelters and busting puppy mills, to sheltering wildlife, to passing legislation that protects some farmed animals from intensive confinement.

Today, HSUS stands as the largest general animal protection charity in the United States. It is also the most politically success-ful animal protection group, having helped to pass hundreds of laws to protect animals over the past few decades. But while most Americans support the sort of legislation HSUS has helped usher in, some industries that use animals have been less than thrilled. In order to fight back and prevent the passage of more animal protection laws, several of these industry groups have called on the assistance of an organization called the Center for Consumer Freedom (CCF).

This shadowy group (its founder, Rick Berman, was publicly denounced by his own son as "a despicable man ... a sort of human molestor [sic]") cut its chops lobbying against drunk driving laws on behalf of the alcohol industry, against anti-smoking initiatives on behalf of the tobacco industry, and against healthy eating measures on behalf of fast-food chains (Landman, 2009). More recently, with the financial support of animal industry groups, CCF has spent huge sums of money publicly attacking HSUS with a barrage of TV, print, public transportation, and online ads. Just what is CCF's main talking point in criticizing the Humane Society? That HSUS does not spend the majority of its budget on the direct rescue and sheltering of animals. In fact, CCF has offered to end its attack ads if the Humane Society agrees to spend more than 50 percent of its budget on hands-on shelter work.

Just why is it that the Humane Society does not spend the majority of its money on rescue and shelter work? And why is it that HSUS would rather weather the storm of CCF's attacks—even though those attacks could result in losing some donor support—than shift the majority of its funding to animal sheltering?

The answer is simple: HSUS can help more animals by focusing most of its money on things other than direct animal care. If HSUS spent every dime on rescuing individual animals, it would be able to help a couple hundred thousand animals per year. But right now, HSUS's legislative and corporate policy victories alone are helping many *millions* of animals per year. So HSUS has chosen to stay the course, in spite of the attack ads funded by industry groups that oppose new animal protection laws. Animals are much better off for HSUS having done so.

This scuffle highlights an important reality in the world of animal protection. Organizations that are effective at addressing the root causes of animal cruelty—things like consumer behavior, corporate policies, and lack of legal protection—help *dramatically* more animals than those focused mainly on direct rescue and sheltering. By comparing the impact of shelter-based organizations with the impact of education- and public policy–based organizations, we can get a glimpse of just how dramatic that difference can be.

By looking through some annual reports, I found that one of the local SPCAs in my area spends about $600 for each dog, cat, or other companion animal that it rescues and re-homes. Certainly $600 is not a bad price for saving a life. A bit more toward the higher end, one of America's more prominent national animal sanctuaries spends over $3,000 per year for each animal under its care. For these organizations, which are roughly representative of shelter and sanctuary groups in general, the "cost per animal helped" runs in the several hundred to several thousand dollar range.

Let's now compare that to the "cost pers" of the top organizations recommended by Animal Charity Evaluators (ACE), an independent charity advisor site that provides guidance to donors who want to help animals. At the time of writing, ACE has spotlighted three top recommended charities on their website, www.animalcharityevaluators.org. One, Mercy for Animals, carries out undercover investigations of factory farms; public education efforts to promote vegetarian eating; legal advocacy work; and corporate advocacy to persuade major food companies to improve the treatment of farmed animals in their supply chain. Another, The Humane League, also carries out public education efforts to promote vegetarian eating, as well as corporate advocacy to persuade food companies and schools to improve the treatment of farmed animals in their supply chain. The third, Animal Equality, carries out undercover investigations in various animal industries; pushes for corporate and legal reforms that benefit animals; and promotes vegetarian eating. None of these three organizations carry out much, if any, direct animal rescue. And all three of them focus exclusively or primarily on farmed animal issues. Interestingly, none of them started out focused mainly on farmed animals, but rather shifted that way over time.

As an important note of disclaimer, I am personally involved with two of these three charities. I work for Mercy for Animals, and I am the founder and a board member of The Humane League. So feel free to assume I could be biased here and to think carefully about any points I'm making instead of just accepting them at face value. It's also worth noting that I am *not* affiliated with Animal Charity Evaluators, the independent organization that reviewed and ranked these and other animal protection charities. For a thorough review of ACE's methodology and data, feel free to visit the Animal Charity Evaluators website.

Anyway, after reviewing the impacts and expenditures of Mercy for Animals, The Humane League, and Animal Equality, ACE concluded that these groups are likely spending *less than a dollar* for each individual animal they help. The help could be significantly reducing an animal's suffering by persuading companies to adopt less-cruel farming systems. The help could also be sparing an animal from being bred and forced to endure a lifetime of extreme misery, accomplished by reducing consumer demand for animal products. While not its own organization, the Humane Society's Farm Animal Protection department is one of several additional organizations spotlighted by ACE as a "Standout Charity." It, too, appears to spend a dollar or less for each animal that it helps.

Recall now that for most rescue- and shelter-focused organizations, the cost per animal helped ranges from several hundred to several thousand dollars per animal. It appears then that certain animal protection charities and approaches can help hundreds to thousands of times more animals than others with each dollar spent.

Whether advocacy-focused and farmed animal–focused organizations also help animals to a greater *degree* than rescue- and shelter-focused organizations is a matter of opinion. If the genie in the bottle popped up again and offered you two new wishes to pick between, which of the following would you choose? Would you rather spare one animal from being born into a lifetime of misery (a frequent goal of farmed animal advocacy work)? Or would you rather allow one animal to live out the remainder of his or her life in comfort (a frequent goal of animal rescue work)?

A straw poll of approximately one hundred animal activists found that, if they had to pick just one, almost 90 percent would choose the first option: to spare one animal from a lifetime of misery. So for most animal activists, the difference in impact between these organizations is even greater than the hundreds- to thousands-fold difference we estimated earlier. (If you personally would prefer to keep an animal alive, the difference would be something less than that, but probably still quite large.)

Earlier in the book we saw that there can be huge differences in impact among charities in different fields, such as the Seva Foundation and the Theatre Communications Group. But is it really possible there could be equally massive differences in impact among charities in the same field? Is it really possible that you could help two animals by donating to one animal protection group, and help two thousand animals by donating to a different group? Even when both of the organizations have a generally sterling public reputation? Even when the people working at both organizations are kind, smart, passionate, friendly, dedicated, wonderful people?

Yes. Not only is it a possibility, it is a reality. While these differences might be particularly vast in the world of animal protection, large differences exist in every field, from environmental advocacy to poverty reduction, from family planning to medical care.

These massive differences reveal just how much is at stake when we donate to one charity instead of another. They reveal just how much is at stake when a non-profit chooses to carry out one program instead of another. Our decisions have life-altering consequences for a huge number of individuals.

While that may sound quite somber, it is also incredibly exciting and empowering. It means that, for those of us who are currently putting money or time into a less-efficient program, we have the power to do so much more good—for animals or for whomever else we may want to help. It means that we as donors, by comparing the "cost per" of similar organizations, can learn how we can bring about tremendously more good with each hard-earned dollar we contribute.

For those of us who work at non-profits, it means that, by comparing the "cost per" of each of our own programs and focusing our spending on the most efficient programs, we can do dramatically more good for our cause. Even groups that are unwilling to make major changes can become more effective. For example, animal sanctuaries and shelters that are unwilling to totally shift their focus can still help exponentially more animals by shifting larger portions of their budget into educational and policy programs that have a dramatically lower cost per animal spared. Even if it continues building homes in the United States, Habitat for Humanity can house many more families by shifting a larger share of its funding overseas. Make-A-Wish could continue granting wishes, and still help tens of thousands more children, by simply moving a fraction of its budget toward more efficient children's health initiatives.

This is the power that following the bottom line can have. It can allow us and the organizations we're involved with to do tens, hundreds, thousands of times more good. All it requires is that we make the effort to follow it, and that we have the self-discipline to act on the sometimes shocking information we learn when we do.

Coming to Grips with the Hard Facts

It can be hard to wrap our brains around the fact that two charities, especially ones in the same field, can have such a vast difference in how successful each is at making the world a better place. It just doesn't *feel* true. For us as donors, choosing to fund one charity versus another, or one program versus another, often feels fairly inconsequential. The emotional pay-off for us is the same either way: we feel good about helping to make the world a better place. So it's hard to grasp the fact that a choice that makes such little difference to us could have such dramatic consequences for the world. It's hard to grasp that writing the name of one charity on a check instead of the name of another charity on a check could have such huge real-world consequences as ten children being stricken with a debilitating disease, one hundred middle-aged women living the remainder of their lives in blindness, or one thousand animals having to undergo a lifetime of torment.

If we could see the individuals we were trying to help, if they lived next door to us or sat in the cubicle next to us at work, it would be far easier to understand how much is at stake with our charity decisions. But for most of us, we are almost never face-to-face with those who benefit from our generosity. Because of that, the difference between helping one child and helping 100 children carries little psychological weight. The importance of helping 600 animals over helping one animal is not emotionally obvious.

That's not the only factor that makes it hard for us to accept what the bottom line tells us and to act on it. A second issue is that doing so could indicate that what we've done in the past has not been the best use of our money, time, or energy. That's a very threatening idea. None of us wants to feel like we've wasted time or money, and none of us wants to feel like we've made less-than-perfect decisions until now.

If accepting these things is tough for a casual donor, it can be nearly impossible for those who work in the non-profit field and who do a type of work that is not particularly high-impact relative to other charities. When we put a lot of effort into something, we become convinced that what we did was worth that effort. It's an unconscious trick of the brain that helps protect us from feeling like we've wasted our time and energy. That's the reason that hazing is so common among fraternities and sororities, and it's part of the reason why boot camp is still an integral part of military training. As unpleasant as these experiences are, those who come out the other side come out with even more commitment to the organization.

So we can probably imagine pretty accurately the reaction that the executive director of the Theatre Communications Group would have to the notion that TCG does exponentially less good for the world than some other charities. We can imagine pretty accurately the reaction of the executive director of the Make-A-Wish Foundation to the suggestion that by shifting a portion of Make-A-Wish's budget to a new program, the organization could do far more good for sick children. We can imagine pretty accurately the reaction of rescue- and shelter-focused animal protection groups to the notion that they could spare far more animals by focusing on consumer education and public policy issues and by focusing on farmed animals instead of cats and dogs.

They—like anyone who is faced with strong evidence that his or her current approach should be changed—would probably find reasons to disagree. Those reasons could take many shapes, from suggesting certain factors have been overlooked, to asserting that a variety of approaches are needed, to disagreeing that the "bottom line" is most important, to arguing that they are just the sort of organization that grants wishes, rescues Labradors, or does whatever they do, and therefore should keep doing that. While the reasons given may vary from person to person, the point is that very few people who work in the charity field would concede that their organization's approach is less effective than other possible approaches.

That's very understandable. It's going to be a touchy subject for any of us who do non-profit work because—while charity is not and should not be about us—it ties in with our sense of self-esteem and competence. That may be part of the reason why we so rarely hear charities or charitable programs compared in this way. Doing so is just, well, impolite. It can hurt feelings. It will certainly make for some awkward and defensive conversations.

Does any charity want to hear that it is a thousand times less effective, or even ten times less effective, than another charity? Of course not. Does any donor want to hear that his or her donation helped three thousand times fewer animals, or even three times fewer animals, than it could have if it were given to a different non-profit in the same field? Of course not. This is surely part of the reason why conversations like the one we're having in this book are so rare.

But if we want to be great at doing good, if we truly want to succeed at making the world a better place, then conversations like these are absolutely vital. They need not be, and are not, a referendum on how compassionate, intelligent, hard-working, or passionate any individual person or any individual organization is. They need not be, and are not, personal, so we have to try as hard as we can to not take them personally.

What they are is an integral part of taking an honest, calculated approach to doing good. They are an unpleasant but necessary exercise that we all have to go through if we want to be more effective at bringing about the better world we want to see.

6

HOW WE CAN DRIVE OUR FAVORITE CHARITIES TO SUCCEED

The $1,500 Bottle of Soda

Imagine that it's 10:30 on a Saturday morning and you're in the grocery store leaning over your shopping cart. You're still in sweatpants and your hair looks a bit of a mess; you're not usually out and about this early on a Saturday morning. Today is different though, because today marks the start of the glorious three-day festival of barbeques and sunshine that is Memorial Day weekend, and you have some serious food shopping to do.

Snacks? Already taken care of. Jammed into one corner of your cart is a mass of shiny crackling bags: tortilla chips, potato chips (regular and the kind with the thick ridges), pretzel rods, popcorn. Produce? Check. Another corner of your cart is piled high with mounds of fresh corn and one of the fattest, juiciest watermelons you've ever seen. Next stop: drinks.

You round the corner and start down the beverage aisle, passing the rows of water (Why buy it when you can get it out of your tap?) and juice (too expensive) before rolling to a stop in front of the soda display case. Row upon row of two-liter soda bottles beam down on you, offering you an array of options for sweet, sugary refreshment. Most of the brands are pretty familiar, but there's an interesting new purple bottle that catches your eye, something you've never seen before. It's called "Crash Cola."

You pick one up and give it a glance-over. As far as you can tell, it's pretty much the same as Pepsi or Coke: just an average run-of-the-mill cola. "Maybe it's a new store brand or something like that," you think to yourself. You're usually a Pepsi drinker, but you hesitate for a second, considering whether or not to give this new cola a try. All of a sudden, your eye catches the price tag.

Whereas most of the two-liter sodas are about $1.50, this one is ... wait, what? That can't be right.

The price tag says "$1,500.00"—that's right, one thousand and five hundred dollars for a two-liter bottle of soda. You start laughing, wondering what brainless stock clerk printed the tag wrong and accidentally set the price at $1,500 instead of $1.50. Pulling out your cell phone you snap a picture; your friends are going to get a laugh out of this.

As you slip the phone back into the pocket of your sweatpants, an actual stock clerk starts walking down the aisle toward you. You start smiling. "Hey, check this out," you say to him. "Your tag says this soda is $1,500. Either someone needs to be re-trained on how to work the label machine, or that's one really expensive bottle of cola!" The stock clerk looks vaguely annoyed, and not at all surprised like you expected him to be.

"Actually, that price tag is correct. That soda is indeed $1,500."

You're about to laugh, but the clerk's face remains vaguely annoyed and a bit impatient. You start to wonder whether he might be serious.

"Wait, you're not serious are you?" you ask him.

"Yes sir, the soda is $1,500. I know it's expensive. Please enjoy your weekend, and thanks for shopping with us." With that, the clerk heads off down the aisle and out of sight.

Standing there with the bottle of Crash Cola in your hand, you don't know what to think. $1,500 for a two-liter bottle of cola? Is that even possible? Slowly you put the bottle back on the shelf. That is one bottle of soda you do not want to accidentally drop on the floor and have to pay for. You look at the price tag for Crash one last time and then turn and grab a bottle of Pepsi. You shake your head, more bewildered than anything else.

"Really?" you think to yourself, "$1,500? Why in the world would anyone pay $1,500 for a generic bottle of soda when they can get Pepsi for a buck fifty? That Crash company is going to go out of business by the end of the week; no one in his right mind would pay that much for soda. I can't believe this grocery store would even stock it."

You would, of course, be right. No one (or at least almost no one) is going to pay a thousand times more than they have to for a bottle of soda. If Crash Cola existed in real life, and was priced that high, the company would be out of business in a heartbeat. That's because in the for-profit world there is an immediate feedback loop between output and income. How much money Crash makes will be directly related to how much value they provide to consumers, relative to other soda companies. Because customers would not be willing to pay anywhere near $1,500 for a bottle of soda, Crash would be doomed.

Buying soda is a pretty straightforward activity. Soda customers want a sugary drink that tastes good, and they don't want to pay a lot for it. Some other things may factor into their decision; for example, they'd probably pay more for a name brand soda like Pepsi or Coke than a generic store brand they'd never heard of. If someone really loved the taste of Crash, she might be willing to pay twice as much, perhaps even three or four times as much, as she would for a Pepsi or a Coke. But there's a limit. Even people who love Crash are not going to pay a thousand times more to buy a Crash instead of a Pepsi.

When a company delivers a lot of value (say, delicious cola) at a competitive price, people will probably buy their product. When a company doesn't deliver a lot of value (say, their cola tastes lousy), or if their price is a lot higher than competitors' prices, people will not buy their product. When that's the case—when a company's product is bad or their price is a lot higher than competitors' prices—the company will fail. People will stop giving them money and they'll go out of business, while the better and cheaper sodas remain on store shelves.

Over the long term this free market competition usually works out very well for customers. Prices go down and the quality of the product goes up. Just look around you; we live in a world where soda is extremely cheap, and—as unhealthy as it may be—it does taste pretty good. This is all thanks to the fact that with soda, as with most basic consumer products, people are pretty clear on what they want. They want a sugary drink that tastes good. They want a fast computer that won't break. They want a basketball that's the right size and weight. And, by and large, they want to spend as little as they can to get it.

The Free Market and the World of Charity

Keeping the free market in mind, let's turn back now to the world of charity. In Chapter 1 we agreed on two premises. First, that the goal of charity is to make the world a better place. It's not to feel good about ourselves or to make things better for ourselves, but to reduce the suffering and increase the well-being of others. Second, we agreed that we want to succeed. We want our charity work to make the world as much of a better place as possible.

If you think about it, what we should want from our charity work is not that different from what we want when we reach for a can of soda. We should want as much value as we can get—that is, we should want to make the world as much of a better place as possible. In addition, we should want to pay as little as we can to get it. We should want our dollar or our hour to stretch as far as possible. That's not because we're stingy; it's because we want our donation or our work to improve the world as much as it can.

To be clear, doing good is not a product. It's not a bottle of soda. But if we want to succeed at charity, then we do want to get as much bang for our buck as we can. The more of it we get, the more individuals who are suffering will receive the help they need. The less bang for our buck we get, the fewer individuals we will be able to help.

You would think that the world of charity would operate like the free market. If it did, donors would give their money to the most efficient charities. They would donate to organizations that produced the most good for the least amount of money—that is, the organizations that improved the world as much as possible per dollar spent. Charities that were extremely efficient would grow very large, their donor base growing and growing as more people learned about the organization and what they do. Extremely inefficient non-profits that required a lot of money to do just a little good—the Crash Colas of the charity world—would not grow, because donors would not want to waste money on them.

In theory, that is what would happen in the non-profit world if donors, like consumers, wanted to get the most bang for their buck. But when we compare charities, whether charities in the same field or charities in general, it becomes very clear that this is not happening. In fact, efficiency doesn't seem to matter at all. There is little to no relationship between how much money a non-profit takes in each year and how much good it does for the world. There is little to no relationship between a charity's output and its income. Non-profits that are extremely efficient at making the world a better place do not see their budgets skyrocketing. Non-profits that are extremely inefficient at making the world a better place do not see their budgets staying small or declining.

Think of the Seva Foundation and the Theatre Communications Group. Based on how most of us prioritized curing people of blindness over improving the quality of the theater arts, we agreed that Seva is probably doing a thousand times more good for the world per dollar spent than TCG. Yet, if we look at the budgets of each organization, we see that they're virtually identical. Donors are putting just as much money toward TCG as they are toward SEVA. In essence, many donors are repeatedly reaching for and buying that $1,500 bottle of Crash Cola, even when an equally delicious $1.50 bottle of Pepsi sits just inches away from it on the shelf.

This doesn't just happen with charities in different fields, it happens with charities in the same field as well. Consider the Schistosomiasis Control Initiative, which we discussed earlier, and another public health related charity, the Cystic Fibrosis Foundation. You'll probably remember that SCI works to combat schistosomiasis, a tropical disease spread by parasitic worms that infects about 200 million people each year. In addition to the short-term impacts it has on everyone who contracts it (bloody stools or urine, stomach cramps, and more), for a portion of the people it infects it can cause lifelong debilitating disease.

We haven't previously introduced the Cystic Fibrosis Foundation, so here's the quick back story. Cystic fibrosis is a rare genetic disorder that affects about 70,000 people around the world, with nearly half of those cases coming from the United States. In people who suffer from cystic fibrosis, a defective gene causes mucus to build up in the lungs and other organs. This buildup leads to inflammation, repeated infections, lung damage, and fatal respiratory failure. There is no known cure for the disease, and it often leads to a premature death. For those who are living with cystic fibrosis, the repeated infections and respiratory issues can be debilitating.

Unfortunately, trying to address cystic fibrosis has been incredibly expensive. The Cystic Fibrosis Foundation (CFF), which was launched back in 1955, currently takes in over $300 million a year to carry out research, treatment, and public education around the disease. Despite the very large budget and the half-century of work, cystic fibrosis has proven to be a very difficult adversary. Thanks to CFF's research and the advancement of specialized care, the average lifespan of someone with cystic fibrosis is a lot longer today than it was in the 1950s. But even so, half of all patients with the disease still die by the age of forty. There is no known cure, and most people stricken with the disease still experience the debilitating health issues described earlier.

While the Cystic Fibrosis Foundation's work is noble, the amount of money it has spent for the amount of good it has done is extremely high. Even if CFF found a complete cure for cystic fibrosis tomorrow, it would have come at a significant price tag: all told, CFF would have spent many hundreds of thousands of dollars for each person spared from this debilitating disease. SCI, meanwhile, spends just $1,000 for each person it spares from a lifetime of debilitating disease.

While both cystic fibrosis and schistosomiasis are very serious problems, it just happens to be the case that the latter is incredibly cheaper to address. You and I can spare many more people from a lifetime of debilitating disease by donating to fight schistosomiasis than we can by donating to fight cystic fibrosis. Therefore, we might expect that the Schistosomiasis Control Initiative would receive at least as much funding as the Cystic Fibrosis Foundation, if not more. After all, wouldn't compassionate donors want to spare more people rather than fewer people from debilitating disease?

Yet SCI's budget is a mere $10 million per year; donors give thirty times more money to the Cystic Fibrosis Foundation than they do to SCI. They do so even though they could help many more people by donating to SCI. (Not that donors know that, of course—we'll get to that point shortly.)

While we could go on and on with many more similar examples, the point is this: when it comes to how much money a non-profit takes in, income is not connected to output. Non-profits that do a lot of good with each dollar spent do not see donations skyrocket. Non-profits that do far less good with each dollar spent do not see donations remain flat or decline. The tragic outcome of this is that the organizations that are most efficient at doing good are not given the resources they need to accomplish all they could. As a result, the world improves a whole lot less than is possible. We as charitable people reduce far less suffering and help far fewer individuals than we have the potential to help.

We can change this. All we have to do is focus our donations on the most efficient charities, those that do the most good per dollar spent. All we have to do is treat charity with at least as much seriousness and straightforwardness as we take buying soda. We look at the options on the shelf. We see where we can receive the most value for the least amount of money. Then we donate accordingly.

When we take this approach, we give great, efficient organizations more of the resources they need to do wonderful things for the world. As if that weren't reason enough to donate that way, there's yet another big benefit to doing so.

Giving Non-Profits the Incentive to Be Great

Do you donate to charity? If so, raise your hand and keep it raised. Now, second question. What is the reason why the amount of money a charity takes in has no relationship to how much good that charity does for the world?

Is your hand still up? I hope so. Because the answer that all of us donors must sheepishly admit is that the reason things are the way they are is because of us. We are the ones funding these organizations. We are the ones donating to non-profits without enough regard for how efficient they are at making the world a better place. We are the ones reaching for the $1,500 bottle of Crash Cola—or a $700 bottle, or a $20 bottle—when a perfectly good $1.50 bottle of Pepsi is sitting right next to it on the shelf. If we're wondering why the great charities don't receive all the money they need and the mediocre charities have more than enough, we have only ourselves to blame.

In 2010 and 2011, the management consultancy firm Hope Consulting carried out a series of large-scale surveys of people who donate to non-profits. These studies, entitled *Money for Good* and *Money for Good II*, focused on households making $80,000 or more per year. The surveys focused on those households because their donations account for three-quarters of all individual charitable giving in the United States. The *Money for Good* surveys polled a grand total of 15,000 individual donors, and the results were, if not surprising, still rather depressing.

Only 3 percent of donors said that how much good a charity does for the world (relative to other charities) was the most important factor when they decided where to donate. Only 6 percent spent any time whatsoever on comparing the impact of different non-profits (Hope Consulting, 2014).

Sure, donors paid plenty of lip service to the importance of how much good a charity is accomplishing. The vast majority said they do care about impact, and one-third of them said they would like to see research that compared different non-profits. But saying and doing are two different things. The sad fact is that right now only a tiny fraction of us are donating based on where we can do the most good. Only a tiny fraction of us are doing anything at all to compare different charities so that we can support the best ones.

In deciding to donate to a hunger relief charity such as Food for Life, very few donors will stop to compare that charity against others before writing a check. Almost no one will try to find out what the cost per child fed is at Food for Life relative to other hunger relief agencies. Almost no one will research long enough to learn that they could feed five malnourished children by donating to one organization or fifty malnourished children by donating to another. Donors just want to support the cause of feeding hungry children. The exact impact they will have is usually given little consideration. We donors may state that we care, but the *Money for Good* studies suggest that very few of us do anything to act on that.

This results in the tragic situation of so much money being more or less wasted. Donor dollars do only a fraction of the good they could be doing, because donors don't seem to care how well their money is used.

There's a second, equally disturbing outcome of all of this. Because we as donors act this way, we have taught charities a horrible lesson: they don't need to worry about how much good they're doing. They don't need to worry about their bottom line or how efficient they are at making the world a better place. We as donors have taught non-profits that, by and large, results don't matter.

Certainly there are exceptions. In some instances non-profits are required to do more in order to receive increased funding from foundations or the government. At times non-profits lose donors or grant money because they have failed dramatically or gone through some very public scandal. Some hyper-efficient charities have been able to successfully attract the attention of the small percentage of donors who really do care about doing as much good as possible. But these are indeed exceptions. On average, there is almost no relationship between how much good a non-profit does and how much money it raises.

With for-profit companies, taking one's eyes off the bottom line of making money is an existential threat. If you're not making money, if you're not selling something of value at a competitive price, you're going to go out of business. But for non-profits, taking one's eyes off the bottom line of making the world a better place is not an existential threat. Even if you're not doing a lot of good, and even if you spend a lot of money for each bit of good you do, you're probably not going to go out of business. As long as you can avoid a huge scandal (for example, spending 80 percent of your budget on fundraising or having your executives convicted of major crimes), and as long as you have some accomplishments you can point to, the money will keep flowing in. Charities know, even if on an unconscious level, that exactly how much good they do for the world does not need to be a big concern.

The sad reality is that there is no financial incentive for non-profits to focus on the bottom line. There is no financial incentive for organizations to try to do more good for the world with each dollar they spend. Charities like Food for Life have no financial incentive to drive down their cost per child fed and help more children. Animal protection groups have no financial incentive to drive down their cost per animal spared by focusing more on public education or policy work. Habitat for Humanity has no financial incentive to drive down its cost per family housed by shifting more of its home-building to developing countries. And when there is no direct incentive to behave a certain way, most people will not behave that way.

"Wait," you may say. "Of course these charities have an incentive to do better. They have an incentive because they care about the issue and they want to help."

Sure, the fact that many non-profit staffers care deeply about the cause they work for means that some of them will indeed be focused on results. Most of them will probably try to not overtly waste money. But keep in mind that non-profit staffers are no different than you and I. If those of us who care deeply about a cause donate with such little concern for the bottom line, should we really expect non-profit staffers to act any differently in their day-to-day work? It would be nice to think that most staffers are keenly focused on the bottom line. It would also be nice to think that most donors are keenly focused on the bottom line. Unfortunately, reality tells us a different story. We need look no further than any of the charities cited in this book—the Make-A-Wish Foundation, Habitat for Humanity, the Cystic Fibrosis Foundation, the Theatre Communications Group, and so on—to realize that most donors and most non-profit staffers are not choosing the path that leads to the greatest good.

While this is all extremely problematic, there is a bright silver lining to the dark cloud. *We can change things.* As donors, each one of us can help lead our favorite charities to greatness by incentivizing them to focus on the bottom line. How can we do that? By being part of the small but growing percentage that does choose where to donate based on how efficient a charity is. By being part of the small but growing percentage that does put in the time to research similar charities to figure out which will accomplish the most good with our donation. The more of us who do this, the more quickly charities will realize that focusing on their bottom line is not just good for the world, it's good for them as well.

Imagine what would happen if the world of charity began to work this way. Imagine if we all took charity in as serious and straightforward a manner as buying soda, and we only donated to the organizations that did the most good for the least amount of money. Non-profits would have an overwhelming financial incentive to succeed at the goal of charity. The same market forces that drive down the price of soda would now drive down the cost of making the world a better place.

Charities that improved the world a lot with each dollar they spent would be rewarded with more and more donations. Charities that ignored the bottom line, and that didn't do much good with each dollar they spent, would remain small or close up shop. As charities doubled down on the bottom line—both to do good and to attract donor attention—their "cost pers" would drop significantly.

Consider what would happen in the field of hunger relief if donors began to donate based on each organization's cost per person spared from hunger (whether that was through direct feeding or through systemic improvements such as agricultural empowerment). Food for Life and every other hunger group would know that, if they wanted to keep their donors, and especially if they wanted to grow as an organization, they would need to have a cost per person spared from hunger that was lower than or at least competitive with the other charities in the field. Food for Life staffers would start calculating their organization's own cost per person spared from hunger and doing their best to learn what that cost was at other groups. They would re-examine every aspect of their program to see how they could drive down the cost. Inefficiencies would be rooted out and removed. Less effective programs would be phased out, and highly effective programs would be ramped up. Very quickly, the cost per person spared from hunger at individual charities and in the field as a whole would drop significantly.

Far more good would be done with each donor dollar. Many more people would be spared from hunger—even if the total amount of money the public donated to hunger relief didn't go up a dime.

The same phenomenon would happen in almost every charitable field. In the field of animal protection, the cost per animal spared would plummet dramatically. Animal charities would realize that if they wanted to obtain more donations and grow as an organization, they would need to focus their work on the issues (such as farmed animals) and approaches (such as education and policy work) that would help the greatest number of animals. Before long, the animal protection field would be helping exponentially more animals each year, even if the total amount of money donated to it didn't increase.

In the environmental protection field, the cost per acre of land protected from development would drop and more land would be protected. In the anti-slavery field, the cost per person freed from labor bondage or sex trafficking would drop and more people would be freed. Multiply this same effect across every charity sector that donors fund. The world would quickly become a much better place.

That is the power that each one of us as donors holds in our hands, or more precisely in our checkbooks and credit cards. We have the power to nudge the entire charity world toward being more effective. Within the specific charitable fields we support, we have the power to nudge non-profits toward feeding more people, protecting more forests, or doing whatever it is they and we are trying to accomplish.

All it requires is that we join the small but growing percentage of thoughtful donors who put their money where it will do the most good. All it requires is that we put in the time to compare charities and figure out which will improve the world the most with our donations, and to have the self-discipline to let that information guide our decisions.

It's Not All Donors' Fault

In the next chapter we'll take a look at some of the psychological reasons why we donors often fail to focus our giving on the charities that do the most good. Before we come to that though, there's a practical hurdle donors face that's worth addressing: most donors simply don't know what works best for creating change. They don't have the time or the data to become experts on which charities and which programs are most efficient.

Is the Against Malaria Foundation or The Bill and Melinda Gates Foundation more effective at reducing the spread of malaria? Will Food for Life or UNICEF feed more hungry people with a $100 donation? Which approach is most likely to succeed at reducing air and water pollution: legislation, litigation, or public education?

Unless we've spent a long time working on the issue, we're probably not going to know the answers to questions like these. Even if we tried to put in the effort to find out, it would be an uphill battle. Since few non-profits take a bottom-line approach, the data we'd need to answer these questions often doesn't exist. When it does exist, it is rarely publicized.

Not knowing what works best isn't always a problem. Consider, for example, the stock market. About half of Americans own stocks, either directly or through mutual or index funds. Yet most of them know next to nothing about the companies they are investing in. They haven't seen the companies' balance sheets or reviewed their quarterly reports. They don't have a grasp for current trends in each company's industry. They probably don't even know the impact that current financial or political events are likely to have on the market as a whole. Because they haven't taken the time to research all this data, most stock-holding Americans would not be able to make smart decisions about which companies are good investments and which are bad investments. Yet they invest anyway, and generally end up making money. How is that possible?

It's possible because most people who invest in the stock market don't pick specific stocks to buy on their own. Because they have a lot at stake—they could either make or lose large sums of money—most individual investors are wise enough to realize the limitations of their knowledge in this area. In fact, financial professionals often warn the public against picking specific stocks on their own. Why? The stock market is tricky. It takes a lot of data and experience before you can reliably perform well and be confident in receiving a good return on your investment when picking your own stocks.

So instead of picking specific stocks themselves, most people either invest in index funds (which is like investing in the stock market as a whole, instead of only certain stocks) or they turn to professionals who can help them accomplish their goals. They use intermediaries like mutual fund managers or full-service stockbrokers. These intermediaries are professionals who have the data and experience to pick specific stocks that are likely to perform well. In exchange for either a set fee or a portion of the profits, they pick which stocks to invest in and then monitor those investments, adjusting when necessary. Because these intermediaries have the data and the experience to make good picks, they usually end up making money for their clients. At every step of the way, clients can examine the returns they're getting and see how much money they're making.

In many ways, the world of the stock market is not that different from the world of charity. Donors are essentially investors; the only difference is that, instead of looking for a financial return on their investment, they are looking for a social return. They want to put money in and get back positive improvements in the world. Just as most individual investors don't know the best ways to pick specific stocks, most donors don't know the best ways to address childhood obesity, homelessness, overpopulation, or any other social issue. Just as individual investors are unlikely to know how well one stock will perform relative to others, donors are unlikely to know how efficient one charity is relative to others.

Ideally, donors would have the same sort of solution to their problem as individual investors have to theirs. Just as investors are able to put their stock picks in the hands of stockbrokers and fund managers, donors could entrust their donation decisions to an intermediary who spends the time and money necessary to develop expertise on a particular charitable sector. These intermediaries could advise donors on which non-profits accomplish the most good per dollar donated, both in specific fields and overall.

Want to donate toward saving rabbits? These donation managers could tell you which rabbit rescue organizations have the lowest cost per rabbit saved, and therefore where you should donate if you want to save as many rabbits as possible. Unsure whether donating to house the homeless or to protect the environment will do more good (based on how much you value each result)? Donation managers could help you compare impact per dollar across fields.

Where would donation managers find the data they'd use to help you make these decisions? Legwork would go a long way. Researching a non-profit's expenses and the exact impact of its programs would give a good sense of how well it was doing at achieving its bottom-line goal. Further, non-profits would feel compelled to collect and share such data because intermediaries would not recommend a charity that hadn't released it. Just as no mutual fund manager would purchase a stock without having concrete financial information about the company (federal law actually requires that publicly traded companies disclose that information), no donation manager would recommend a charity unless concrete information on that charity's impact was publicly available.

Unfortunately, intermediaries like these do not exist in the non-profit world. While there may be several reasons for this, one possible conclusion seems unavoidable: we do not take charity as seriously as we take making money. We do not take helping others as seriously as we take helping ourselves.

Mutual fund managers and full service stockbrokers open up shop because there is a market for their services. Investors care enough about making money that they will pay brokers and managers to make the right decisions for them. If we took charity just as seriously, there would also be a market for intermediaries to guide donor dollars. Since donation managers like these don't exist, it seems that this is a service the public does not care enough to pay for. On the other hand, it is possible that, were such intermediaries to set up shop, donors and foundations would be willing to pay for their services. Since this has never been tried, donors may not even realize it could be an option.

Unhelpful Advice

That's not to say there are no intermediaries at all between donors and non-profits. There are a few. Some financial planning firms are staffed with philanthropic advisors who help clients set up foundations, decide which non-profits to support, and so forth. Unfortunately, the goal of these advisors is not to show clients where they can achieve the most good per dollar donated. In fact, the *Money for Good* studies found that philanthropic advisors are just as unlikely as individual donors to see a non-profit's impact as the most important factor in deciding which charities to recommend. Fewer than 5 percent of philanthropic advisors recommend charities based on how much good they do. Because clients aren't interested in that sort of information, philanthropic advisors don't provide it. They simply connect a client with respected and financially sound non-profits in the client's areas of interest and help with handling the transfer of funds.

In addition to philanthropic advisors, there are moderately well-known websites such as CharityNavigator.org, Guidestar.org, and MyPhilanthropedia.org (which is owned by Guidestar) that exist to help donors make more informed donor decisions. Some of these sites even provide ratings or rankings for various charities. Sites like these *could* be, and perhaps one day will be, incredibly useful sources of information for donors. But at the moment the information they provide and the ranking systems they use have nothing or almost nothing to do with how successful non-profits actually are at making the world a better place.

On the information side, Guidestar and Charity Navigator provide financial breakdowns from charities' annual filings with the IRS. You can view the expenses and revenue of organizations, see how much they spent on fundraising and administration, find out who the top executives are and what they are paid, and learn the basics about the programs they carry out.

It's good that all of this information is made available, but the problem is that it tells us almost nothing about how successful a charity is at achieving its bottom-line goal. How many acres of rainforest are conserved, how many unwanted pregnancies are prevented, how many homeless veterans receive services for each donor dollar? Guidestar and Charity Navigator don't have and therefore don't provide that information. Since they don't, what people who use these sites pay attention to, and what they think they should be paying attention to, are things like how much an organization spends on overhead, how much top executives are paid, and how transparent an organization is with its financial and board information. The *Money for Good* surveys found that overhead—the percentage of its budget an organization spends on fundraising and administration—is the number one thing donors look for when researching a charity.

But here's the thing about overhead, salaries, and transparency. Looking at those figures can tell you whether the charity you're thinking of donating toward is scandalously horrible. These scam-style non-profits are the ones that spend eighty or ninety cents of every dollar you donate on professional fundraising fees, that pay their executive director an annual salary of $500,000 when the entire organization's budget is only $2 million, or that are misusing funds for their own personal benefit. In fact, that is why most donors look at these figures.

Money for Good found that, among donors who did any research before writing a check, most of them were simply trying to confirm that a charity they planned to donate toward did not have something particularly wrong with it.

But for the 98 percent of charities that aren't scandalously bad, looking at overhead, salaries, and transparency will tell us very little about how much good they do or about how they compare to similar charities. Consider the Seva Foundation and the Theatre Communications Group. Imagine that, in addition to everything I told you about Seva earlier, I also told you that it spends 60 percent of its budget on overhead and only 40 percent on programs. Or imagine that I told you its executive director makes $400,000 a year. Or that its board has only four members and that it's not as open about disclosing financial information as most non-profits are. (Note that I am making all of these things up for purposes of this example. These are fictitious numbers.) Imagine that, by contrast, TCG spent just 5 percent of its budget on fundraising, that its executive director took just a $20,000 salary, that its board was staffed with a wide array of talented and respected people, and that it completely disclosed every single line item of its finances.

If the above were true, we might dislike some or all of those things about Seva. We might think it's unethical for their executive director to be paid so much. We might think it's excessive for Seva to put so much of each donor's dollar into overhead. We might think it's admirable that the Theatre Communication Group's executive director makes so little, and be impressed by the size and caliber of TCG's board.

But regardless of our opinions on those things, none of it would change the fact that we would still accomplish a thousand times more good for the world by donating to Seva than we would by donating to the Theatre Communications Group. Regardless of what overhead, salaries, and transparency policies we may find at each organization, the bottom-line results each organization has for the world would still the same as they were before. If we want to make the world as much of a better place as possible, if we want to help as many individuals as possible, that bottom line is what matters most.

Donors have been taught, in part by sites like Charity Navigator and Guidestar, to focus on how much a charity spends on overhead. Organizations with a high overhead are considered inefficient, and organizations with a low overhead are considered efficient. But the reality is that overhead usually has very little to do with how efficient a charity is. Why? Because the biggest inefficiencies lie somewhere we don't even think to look: within the program budget.

It doesn't matter that a charity is putting 95 percent of its money into programs if the programs it's running are not very efficient. Some programs are exponentially more efficient than others. Some programs will house ten times more families, help hundreds of times more sick kids, and, in general, do dramatically more good per dollar spent than other programs. These differences between programs are so massive that the percentage a non-profit spends on overhead is almost irrelevant. The only exception is the rare non-profit that spends almost every penny on overhead.

That doesn't mean we can't or shouldn't encourage non-profits to avoid exorbitant salaries, refrain from wasting money on ineffective fundraising, be more transparent with their financials, and so forth. We can and often should do all of those things. But the point remains that by focusing on overhead, salaries, transparency, and anything else other than how much good a non-profit does for the world per dollar donated, we are missing the forest for the trees.

While Guidestar does not rank charities, Charity Navigator provides a rating of 1 to 100, as well as a corresponding star rating of zero to four stars, for thousands of charities that it has reviewed. Unfortunately, the rankings suffer from the same problem as the information portion of the site: they are not focused on how effective a charity is at making the world a better place. Instead, its rankings are based exclusively on things like a charity's financial performance, its overhead, how much financial and governance information it provides on its website and in its tax return, and so forth. As we've noted, while these things are interesting, they don't tell us much about how successful a non-profit is at making the world a better place.

Consider, for example, Charity Navigator's ratings of hundreds of animal protection charities. When we discussed animal protection earlier, we spoke about how there's a pretty obvious bottom-line goal for animal protection groups. Their bottom line is to help animals. The greater the number of animals they help, and the greater the degree of help they provide to each animal, the more successful they are.

If we look at Charity Navigator's rankings of animal protection groups though, we see that there is no relationship between the rating given to an animal protection charity and how many animals that charity helps. Organizations that provide a lot of help to a lot of animals at a very low cost do not necessarily receive good ratings. Organizations that provide a modest amount of help to a tiny handful of animals at a very high cost do not necessarily receive low ratings. Within Charity Navigator's rankings are numerous charities that helped hundreds of thousands or even millions of animals in the previous year but that are given low ratings because certain items aren't posted on their website, or because the group's board of directors is not large enough to be ideal. Meanwhile, many charities that helped only a few hundred animals the previous year, and at a very large cost, receive four-star ratings.

When we look at human health charities, we see the same thing. There is little to no relationship between the rating given to a charity and how many sick people the charity has helped or how many sick people the charity helped per dollar donated. Equally misleading ratings exist for charities in every field, from poverty reduction to education to environmental protection.

Because of this, Charity Navigator's ratings give donors very little useful information about which charities are worth supporting. In fact, the ratings probably do more harm than good because they encourage donors to focus on the wrong criterion. Donors would be better off just picking charity names out of a hat.

If at some point sites like Guidestar and Charity Navigator begin to stress to donors that impact matters most, and if they begin to provide bottom-line data so donors can compare organizations against one another on their "cost pers," sites like these could become incredible forces for good. It's worth noting that Charity Navigator has announced plans to start including "results reporting" on its website in the next couple of years. Their stated plan is to gather whatever available data they can about the actual impact of the charities in their database and to use that information as part of their ratings process. It remains to be seen when and how Charity Navigator implements results reporting. If they execute it well, provide bottom-line information to donors, and begin to base their ratings on exactly how much good an organization has done per dollar spent, Charity Navigator could become an invaluable resource. Unless and until that happens though, it and other sites like it will be of only marginal use to donors.

A New Breed of Charity Advisors

In the meanwhile, a few more thoughtful competitors in the charity-ranking world have begun to move the ball forward in providing donors with bottom-line information on certain charities. For example, the website GiveWell.org sorts through a large number of anti-poverty and human health charities to identify those that produce, in GiveWell's ethical worldview, the most good per dollar donated. Reports on the top recommended charities include a rigorous analysis of each organization's bottom line, the cost per successful intervention, a review of strengths and weaknesses, and a projection of how much additional funding the organization could receive before it began to decline in cost-effectiveness.

Unavoidably, the recommendations GiveWell makes reflect the organization's own ethics. Its recommendations suggest that its founders prioritize saving human beings from dying (mainly of disease) and trying to reduce extreme global poverty. You or I may have different priorities. We may value other things more highly. There may be things we value less highly but that are a whole lot cheaper to bring about. We may balk when we consider the long-term impacts that donating to these sorts of charities could have. The point is that we are not necessarily going to come to the same conclusions as GiveWell when deciding what the best places to donate toward are.

But this is not a criticism of the website; every site that ranks charities is going to do so based on its own value system. GiveWell should be applauded for basing its rankings on a clear bottom-line goal and for encouraging donors to focus on exactly what results a charity will bring about with each dollar donated.

AnimalCharityEvaluators.org, which we mentioned earlier, provides a similar analysis of the most cost-effective animal protection charities in the United States. Out of the tens of thousands of animal charities that exist, ACE selected one hundred for consideration based on the scope of each charity's work and their likelihood of being among the most effective. After an initial review of those hundred, ACE conducted in-depth interviews with and research on a smaller number of organizations to try to quantify the number of animals each organization had helped, how much those animals had been helped, and how much money was spent to do so. In the end, ACE recommended three charities, The Humane League, Mercy for Animals, and Animal Equality, as the organizations accomplishing the most good for animals with each dollar donated.

Just as with GiveWell, the recommendations that Animal Charity Evaluators makes reflect its own ethical worldview. ACE prioritizes either saving the life of an animal or preventing or reducing the extreme suffering of an animal. Also, they don't differentiate based on species. That is, Animal Charity Evaluators doesn't view sparing a dog from abuse as any more or less valuable than sparing a panda bear or a pig from the same sort of abuse. That approach certainly makes a lot of sense if our goal is to reduce suffering and increase well-being. Just as feeding a hungry child does equal good whether the child lives in India or in Kansas, sparing an animal from misery does roughly equal good whether the animal is a rabbit or a chicken.

Sites such as AnimalCharityEvaluators.org and GiveWell.org are setting good models for how donors should think about which charities to support. Much like stockbrokers, or even sales clerks in the soda aisle, they are giving donors practical, concrete information about what they can accomplish with their donations and where they can donate to get the most bang for their buck. They are providing the data we donors need to achieve our goal of making the world as much of a better place as possible.

7

OUR BRAINS DON'T WANT US TO BE GREAT AT DOING GOOD, BUT WE CAN OUTSMART THEM

What Charity Looks Like on the Inside

In 2006, researchers at the National Institutes of Health in Bethesda, Maryland, had some questions about what it really means to do good. They wanted to know what things look like in the brain of a person who is donating to charity. What mental processes are going on when we decide to give money to a cause we support?

To find out, they teamed up with researchers at the University of Genoa Medical School in Italy as well as researchers at two institutes in Brazil to carry out an experiment. Participants were recruited, and on the day of the experiment each person was inserted into an fMRI machine to undergo the study.

In case you're not familiar with what an fMRI is and how it works, the machine itself looks kind of like a big fat mechanical donut. A person's head slides into the hole in the middle and remains there during the course of the experiment. The function of the machine is to tell which parts of the brain a person is using at any given time. The way it does this is by using magnetic imaging to watch how blood flows through the brain.

Each region of the brain is associated with one or more different mental processes. For example, when we're feeling empathy for someone, the region of our brain that's associated with empathy jumps into action. Blood flow to the area increases. By watching where the blood is flowing, fMRI machines can track which parts of the brain are associated with different emotions, thought processes, and so forth. In this case, scientists wanted to see which parts of the brain light up when people make charitable decisions.

Once participants were safely tucked inside the donut hole of the fMRI machine, they were told they would be given up to $130. If they wanted to keep it all, they could keep it all. But they would also be given a number of opportunities to donate portions of it to various real charities. These included charities that worked on the issues of abortion, the death penalty, nuclear proliferation, gender equality, euthanasia, and child protection.

Participants were presented with a variety of scenarios and questions around the money. In some situations, they were simply asked whether they wanted to receive a small amount of money, such as $2. In others, they were asked whether they would rather receive money or have money go a particular charity. In still other situations, they were given the chance to provide a charity with money that didn't come out of their own pockets. While all of this was going on, the fMRI machine kept track of which regions of their brains were being activated.

What the machine found was that when participants were given money by researchers, the reward center of their brains—the part associated with anticipating and receiving pleasure from sex, food, and drugs—was activated. People felt good about receiving free money. But when participants were giving some of that money back to charity, the reward center of their brain was also activated. In other words, giving to charity provided a dose of pleasure through much the same brain channels as having sex or receiving money. On top of that, donating to charity also activated a second reward center in the brain, one involved with the positive feelings that come from strong social attachments.

The other key thing researchers found had to do with the front end of a section of our brain called the prefrontal cortex. If you poke yourself in the middle of your forehead, you'll be pointing right at this part of your brain. The National Institutes of Health study found that when people had a costly decision to make—for example, when the donation they were considering was large—the prefrontal cortex sprang into action. It tried to assist with the decision making when self-interest and ethical beliefs seemed to be at odds.

Subsequent fMRI studies by other teams have continued to find that, when we donate to charity, the reward centers of our brains are activated. In fact, even when we give to the greater good involuntarily—for example, through being taxed—we receive at least some reward in the same parts of our brains.

In summary, what scientists have found is that giving to charity is often an inherently pleasurable act. It makes us feel rewarded in two different parts of our brains: the part through which sex, drugs, food, and money make us feel good and the part associated with being connected to others. When doing good seems like more sacrifice than reward—for example, when we're asked to donate a lot of money, or perhaps when we're asked to donate toward something we know is good but that doesn't have a big emotional payoff—we're stuck. Our prefrontal cortex steps in to help us make a decision. In that regard, we might think of the prefrontal cortex as an enlightened scale. It tries to get us to base our decisions not just on what the immediate reward is for us, but also on what is best for bringing about the world we want to see.

Questioning Our Motives

The reason for our short diversion into the field of neuroscience is this. If someone asked you why you do donate or volunteer, what would you say? Most of us would probably say we do it because we want to give back, we want to make a difference, it's the right thing to do, or something else along those lines. Most of us also really do care about the causes we donate to or work on.

But that altruistic motivation isn't the only thing driving us to do good. We also do good because it feels good. It rewards us in much the same way that sex, food, and friendship can reward us. Just as the desire for these other short-term rewards can lead us to make less-than-stellar decisions (Is eating that huge tub of French fries really worth it? Is sleeping with your secretary really a good idea?), the desire to feel good from doing good can also lead us to make poor charity decisions. In craving the "warm glow" feeling that can come from doing good, we may make charity decisions that feel great to us but that don't do very much for the world.

Donating $100 to help a specific cute little girl in our town whose adorable picture we saw, whose name we know, and whose story was just on the news would probably feel incredibly great. It would light up those reward centers of our brain like Times Square at night. (If you've never been to Times Square at night, to say it's bright would be an understatement.) On the other hand, donating $100 to help five Brazilian children whose names we don't know, whom we will never see, whose specific story we haven't heard, and who live in a country we've never been to, is not going to have the same emotional pay-off. For most of us, it's not going to light up those reward centers of our brain much at all.

But what is our goal in donating? Is our goal to benefit ourselves by igniting those reward centers of our brain and feeling the same rush we get from steamy sex, mouthwatering meals, and hanging out with friends? Or is our goal to help children in need? If our goal is to light up our own pleasure centers while at the same time doing a little good, we should donate to help the one American girl whose story we know. If our goal is to help children in need, we should donate to help the five Brazilian children.

We saw earlier that the amount of good a charity does for the world has almost no relationship to how much money donors give to it. A small part of the reason for this is that donors don't necessarily know which charities are most effective. But the bigger reason is that, as was made clear in the *Money for Good* surveys, most donors don't base their decisions on a charity's impact. How much good a donation will do for the world is not the main concern. That suggests that many of us have a different main concern: how good our donations will make us feel.

If we are donating to a children's health charity, is our main priority to protect children from the misery of disease? Or is our main priority to light up the reward centers of our brains, while at the same time doing something, however large or small, that helps protect children? For those of us who donate to the theater, is our main priority really to make the world a better place? Or is our main priority to light up the reward centers of our brain that are associated with charitable giving, while at the same time doing something, however large or small, that benefits society? This may seem like a minor difference, but the consequences are enormous. If our main priority is not helping others, if it is not making the world as much of a better place as possible, then as a charitable people we will fall far, far short of our potential to do good.

Of course, there's nothing wrong with feeling good about doing good. We should feel good about helping others. If that feeling helps propel us to provide more and more support to great causes, then that's wonderful. The question is in where our priorities lie. If we want to be great at doing good, charity should be an area of our lives in which helping others is always the top priority and firing up the reward centers of our brains is always a very distant second. That doesn't mean we have to be perfect saints. Remember that charity takes up only a small slice of each of our lives. We can take a totally altruistic approach to charity and still have huge portions of our lives in which we make ourselves the number one priority, if that's what we want to do.

Right now, though, the fMRI studies, the *Money for Good* surveys, and our charitable giving patterns suggest something that is not very flattering about us donors overall. They suggest that our desire to feel good can lead us to make less-than-ideal decisions when trying to do good. They suggest that in many ways our charitable decisions may be more about feeling good than they are about doing good.

Looking Out for Number One, in More Ways Than One

The desire to light up the mental reward centers of our brains isn't the only personal motivation that can influence our charity decisions. We are all human, so we all have a slew of needs and desires that we want to satisfy. Each one of these has the potential to steer us toward focusing more on ourselves than on helping others, even when we're trying to do good.

We all have the desire to feel good about ourselves, to be accepted by others, to express ourselves, and to validate our worldview as correct. We want to feel important, to have mastery of some skill, to spend time doing the things we enjoy doing, and to live comfortably. All of these desires are well and good. They're a natural part of being a happy, healthy human being. But we should notice that, when our altruistic goal of making the world a better place seems to conflict with one of these personal goals, our inclination is almost always to side with ourselves, to do what's best for us. If we don't watch out for this, if we don't notice when it's happening and try to correct it, it can lead us to make charity decisions that are out of sync with our goal of making the world a better place.

Consider, for example, the following scenarios for donors:

- Imagine you received social condemnation instead of social approval for donating. For example, your parents and friends would be angry with you if you gave money to charity. The newspapers and nightly news occasionally run stories arguing that we shouldn't be trying to help others and that donating to charity is not something respectable people did. Television sitcoms and stand-up comedians playfully mock those who donated to charity as silly, idealistic fools. If this were the world you lived in, would you continue volunteering or donating to charity? Would you donate as much as you do now?

- Imagine you donate to a charity in your city that promotes literacy by helping those who are illiterate learn to read. You also occasionally volunteer, and you're friends with everyone who works there. You then learn that an organization that promotes literacy in rural India is doing amazing work. They are able to help people learn how to read quickly and at a low cost, and there is rampant illiteracy in the rural areas they work in. You only have enough money to donate to one charity. Do you continue donating to the local charity you volunteer with, or do you donate to the charity in India where it will likely help more people?

- Imagine that you see a television news report about the ongoing problem of human slavery and labor trafficking around the world. Shocked that this is still going on, you decide you want to make a generous donation to help stop it. How likely do you think you would be to spend a good amount of time—say six hours or more—to thoroughly investigate which charity in that field would do the most good with your donation?

In each of these situations, our altruistic desire to do good comes into conflict with our personal desires. This may be the desire to feel approval from our friends and society, to support causes that we have a personal connection with, or not to have to spend our time doing research when we could be doing something fun instead. In each scenario, we see the incredibly strong tug that our personal desires can have over our charitable decisions. They can lead us away from what will do the most good and toward what is easiest or most rewarding for us.

Consider a few more examples, this time for those who work as non-profit staffers:

- Imagine that you work at the Make-A-Wish Foundation. You have the idea that the Foundation should start a new program called "Wish to Be Well" that funds efforts to spare children in Africa and Asia from the debilitating effects of an easily treatable tropical disease. Starting the program would mean taking some money away from the wish-granting work that your organization does. It would also mean breaking entirely new ground, since Make-A-Wish has never done anything other than grant wishes for the thirty years it's been in existence. You know that you will invoke the anger or disdain of most of your colleagues if you push for this new program, but it seems pretty clear to you that Make-A-Wish will be able to help more children if the program is created. Would you lobby hard for the new program, even in the face of disdain from your co-workers?

- Imagine that you care deeply about protecting the environment, and you're about to take a job at an environmental protection non-profit that you think does really great work. They make you a salary offer of $50,000. Your spouse has a job that pays well, so you know that your family could get by just fine, even if your new salary were as low as $20,000 or $25,000. Would you tell your new employer that you'd like a significantly lower salary so that the organization can put that extra money into its programs?

Again, we see how our minds seem pre-set to always try to pull us in the direction of doing what's best for us, even when it's to the detriment of a cause we care passionately about.

For those of us who do work at non-profits, it isn't just a desire to do what's best for ourselves that can pull us in the wrong direction. Wanting to do what's best for our group can have the same effect.

We humans are social animals. For most of our existence, we lived in small tribes that hunted, procreated, traveled, and at times went into battle together. Group survival and individual survival were one and the same. That pack mentality survives to this day, with the groups we belong to still being an integral part of our self-identity. For example, I might be an Oakland

Raiders fan, a Chicago native, an Irish descendant, or a Roman Catholic. I could be a techie or a cheerleader or a Republican. These group memberships have a strong influence on how I see myself, how I see others, and how I experience life. They become a part of who I am. When the Raiders lose a game, I am dejected. When the Republicans take control of the House and Senate, I feel jubilant.

The same tribal mentality kicks into gear when we go to work at a non-profit organization. We become proud staffers of the American Red Cross or the United Way or Doctors Without Borders. The groups we work for become part of our self-identity, and just like Raiders fans, our emotions can start to rise and fall in response to the triumphs and setbacks of our organization. There are some positive consequences to this. It can motivate us to work harder, for example, because when the organization succeeds we feel that we have succeeded. But there is at least one big negative consequence of identifying with the group we work for: it can lead us to prioritize the good of the organization over the good of the cause we're trying to advance. It's a sort of second-degree self-centeredness; we prioritize helping the group because it has become a part of who we are.

Consider these last two examples:

- Imagine that you work for the World Wildlife Fund. You took a job there as vice president several years ago because you really care about protecting wild animals and their habitat. You also find it's an enjoyable place to work; you're treated well as a VP, and you like your co-workers.
  One night at a cocktail party you end up chatting with a very wealthy businesswoman. When she finds out you work at WWF, she tells you that she's very bothered by the impact the human race is having on the rest of the planet. She's been planning to donate $1 million to a wildlife protection organization, but she hasn't decided which one yet. She asks whether WWF would be a good place to donate to.

What do you tell her? Do you encourage her to donate to the World Wildlife Fund and start describing all of the exciting programs your organization is carrying out to try to solidify her interest? Or do you think about the wildlife conservation field as a whole and then recommend the charity that you honestly think would do the most to help wild animals with her million dollars? Keep in mind that there are hundreds of charities in the field. The odds are very unlikely that the group you work for just happens to be the group that would do the most good with her donation.

- Imagine you're an employee at the human rights organization Amnesty International. A colleague at a charity called Tostan, which also works on human rights issues, sends you an email asking for your help with an urgent project he's working on. It sounds like it would have a really great impact if it succeeds. Your colleague asks you to put aside what you're doing at Amnesty International for the next couple weeks and instead just spend your time helping Tostan (for free) until the project is done.
  How would you respond? Would you say that you have to focus on your own work and do what you're paid to do at Amnesty International, even if that work has less of a payoff? Or would you agree to help? If you asked your supervisor at Amnesty International for permission, what do you think she or he would say?

Scenarios like these merely scratch the surface of how decisions that seem obvious are not always so obvious when we stop to think more carefully about what's best for the cause we're supporting. Almost all of us are hard-wired to favor benefits to ourselves or our organizations over major, even lifesaving benefits to those we want to help. Because it happens on such an instinctual level, we rarely even notice what's going on. Only by paying close attention to the outcome can we realize how many of our seemingly innocuous charity decisions could actually hurt the very cause we care so deeply about.

While this chapter has been mostly doom and gloom so far, don't worry. In a little bit we'll talk about how we can take the self-centered tendencies we all have and actually put them to use for making the world a better place. Before we do though, we need to dive a little deeper into the murky depths of our minds. There are still more ways in which our brains seem to be conspiring to trip us up when we're trying to do good.

Our Biases Try to Rule Us, and This One Is Really Bad

Looking out for number one is just one of several psychological biases that can lead us to make poor decisions when trying to do good. Like the focus on ourselves, these other biases probably exist because they gave our ancestors some evolutionary advantage. But as we'll see, traits that helped our ancestors survive and reproduce are not necessarily traits that will help us make smart charity decisions.

A second major bias we all have that can really stand in the way of doing good is our tendency to care more about those who are similar to us. This has been a problem throughout the ages: tribes going to battle against other tribes, competing religious sects committing atrocities against one another, certain races enslaving other races, and countries doing battle against one another in wars that end millions of lives. We can see the same phenomenon on a smaller scale in our own lives. Consider the sense of camaraderie we immediately feel for those who attended the same college as we did and how much more we care about our family members than we do about strangers we pass on the street. This bias to care more about those who are similar to us also spills over into the charity decisions we make.

We'd probably all agree that, if our empathy was logical, it wouldn't matter what the color of a person's skin happened to be when it came to lending a helping hand. A person is a person. If he or she is in need, we ought to care just as much about the person whether he or she is pale white, dark brown, or anything in between. While that's what most of us would say we believe, our bodies tell a different story. Studies have found that, even on neural and physiological levels, we care more about those who are the same race as we are.

In one study, participants were put into an fMRI machine and shown images of people who were suffering. When the people in the photos were the same race as the participant, the participant had a much stronger empathetic response. The areas of the brain that have to do with compassion and caring lit up more brightly. When a participant was shown pictures of people who weren't the same race as he or she was, those areas of the brain were not activated as strongly. This bias didn't just travel in one racial direction; for example African-Americans had a more empathetic response when they saw African-Americans who were suffering, and Caucasian participants had a more empathetic response when they saw Caucasians who were suffering. It seems as if evolution has rigged our brains to make us care more about those who are similar to us. This bias happens on an immediate, instinctual level, even before we reach the realm of conscious decision making.

Of course, in the world of conscious decision making, the tendency to care more about those who are similar to us continues. We read and watch news about what's happening in our community and our country, but most of us pay little attention to foreign news unless what's going on is particularly dramatic or could affect our country. We're shocked and horrified by terrorism at home (consider the 9/11 attacks and the Boston Marathon bombing), but only minimally bothered by terrorist attacks in India, Somalia, and elsewhere. Urbanites sometimes look with mild disdain on rural America, and rural America sometimes looks back with mild disdain on city-dwellers. Politicians lobby for pork barrel spending that benefits their districts, even when it comes at the expense of other parts of the country, and their constituents re-elect them for having done so.

The bias to care more about those who are similar to us spills over to the world of charity as well. Consider the many walks and runs held to raise money to fight breast cancer, AIDS, lymphoma, and other diseases. Many of the people taking part in these walks have family members who suffer or suffered from the disease. All of us are much more likely to take action against a problem, health-related or otherwise, that affects someone close to or similar to us.

It's great that knowing someone with a disease can motivate us to take action against it. The downside is that it predisposes us to ignore very serious issues that don't affect those who are close to or similar to us. For example, how many walks or runs against schistosomiasis have you heard about in your city? Probably none. If schistosomiasis was common in the United States though, and if many of us had a friend or relative who has contracted it, the issue would undoubtedly generate a huge amount of funding and public concern.

For another example, consider the fact that, although there are many malnourished people in the United States, there are far more people suffering far worse malnutrition in places like Africa and Asia. Nevertheless, the majority of food assistance funded by Americans goes to other Americans. Why? Because they look like us, live near us, and are members of our socio-political group. So our brains tell us to care more about them—even though people outside of America are in far greater need. In virtually every charitable field, Americans give much more money to non-profits that focus on America than to those whose programs are focused on other countries.

Our innate tendency to act this way is often rationalized by statements that we need to take care of ourselves first before we can take care of others. But when it comes to doing good, the logic just doesn't hold. If our goal is to reduce suffering and increase well-being, it doesn't make much difference where on the globe that's taking place and who is experiencing it. In 1963, President John F. Kennedy famously declared to a crowd of 450,000 West German citizens, "Ich bin ein Berliner" (or "I am a Berliner") to show American solidarity for democratic West Germany. "All free men, wherever they may live, are citizens of Berlin," added Kennedy (Kennedy, 1963). If we want to be great at doing good, we would do well to act in the same spirit. Wherever someone is suffering and in need, he or she is already one of us.

With that sentiment in mind, let's also now consider how our innate bias to care more about those who are similar to us doesn't just influence our treatment of individuals who are a different race, sex, or nationality than the one we happen to be. It also influences our treatment of individuals who are a different species than the one we happen to be.

Studies have shown that, both on a physiological level and in our attitudes, we have widely varying levels of empathy for non-human animals. How much empathy we have depends in part on which species an animal is. The closer a species is to ours in the evolutionary tree, the more we tend to care about members of that species. For example, tests have found that we have more of an empathic response to primates who are suffering than we do to large mammals like pigs and cows who are suffering. We have more empathy for pigs and cows than we do for birds such as chickens. Well below even chickens come fish and other "lesser" creatures, many of which generate little to no empathic concern.

Our empathy doesn't have much do with how capable an animal is of feeling pain or experiencing pleasure. A chicken, for example, is able to feel pain and pleasure in much the same way as a monkey. What our empathy does seem to correlate to is how similar an animal's species is to our own. The closer they are to humans on the evolutionary tree, the more we tend to care about them. Our empathy also has a lot to do with how familiar and emotionally close to us that species of animal is. Societies that care for cats or dogs in their homes usually grow to have much more empathy for them than for other species. Because they share our homes and our lives, we have come to view cats and dogs as "one of us."

Our bias toward caring more about species that we perceive as similar to us has several big impacts when it comes to charity. The first is that, of the money that is donated to animal charities, the vast majority is used to help the species that are most familiar and close to us: cats and dogs. But other types of animals, particularly farmed animals, suffer much more intensely and in far greater numbers than companion animals. While there are several million cats and dogs euthanized each year due to lack of a home in the United States, there are nine billion pigs, chickens, and other farmed animals each year that spend their entire lives packed in filthy, disease-ridden warehouses.

The second and more overarching result of our bias toward helping those who are similar to us is that many of us have never even considered donating to help animals in the first place. In case you're not familiar with the ways in which animals are abused, and since this is an issue near and dear to me, allow me one paragraph to explain how animals such as farmed animals are treated.

Pigs, cows, chickens, and other farmed animals are often crammed in pens so small they literally cannot turn around or can only barely do so. Imagine locking your dog in a tiny dog crate and leaving him there for the next two years. That is the sort of physical and mental experience that many farmed animals endure. Many live their whole lives on painful wire caging or feces-filled concrete floors. Broken bones and gaping wounds are common, and sick animals receive no veterinary attention. Because they can't lay eggs and are therefore not profitable, male chicks are tossed alive into giant grinding machines at just a few days old. Piglets that don't grow fast enough are killed by being slammed headfirst into the concrete floor. Teeth, testicles, and tails are cut off without anesthesia. Common ways of dying at the slaughterhouse include having your throat slit, being scalded to death in a tank of burning hot water, and having a metal rod shot through your brain. All of these practices are both standard and perfectly legal, since animal cruelty laws specifically exclude farmed animals from protection.

The point of sharing that gut-wrenching description is this. Since the goal of charity is to make the world a better place by reducing suffering and increasing well-being, it's worth keeping in mind the staggering amount of suffering endured by non-human animals. It's also worth keeping in mind that the cost of helping them can be mind-bogglingly cheap. As we saw earlier, it can cost less than a dollar for a very effective charity to spare one farmed animal from the lifetime of intense misery described in the last paragraph.

If we want to succeed at the goal of charity—decreasing suffering and increasing well-being as much as possible—we should consider this an area where we can achieve an incredibly large bang for our charitable buck. Of course, doing so requires overcoming the strong pre-programming our brains have to care little about those who seem dissimilar to us. It may also require giving money to individuals who we feel little instinctual empathy for, at least initially.

Regardless of how you feel about animal issues, the situation illustrates just how much of an impact our innate psychological biases can have on the charity decisions we make. It illustrates how far short of our potential we can fall when we let those biases toward helping those similar to us guide our decisions, be it on animal protection issues or on any other charitable cause.

Empathy and Evolution

Perhaps it shouldn't be a surprise that we are biased to care more about those who are similar to us or close to us. After all, evolution didn't one day decide to stick empathy and kindness in us so we could make the world a wonderful place. These traits evolved because they helped us pass on genes. On a biological level they exist for that purpose. So we should expect our charitable instincts to focus on individuals who are genetically similar to us, geographically close to us, and psychologically familiar to us. Those are the individuals most likely to share our genes. They are also the ones most likely to return a favor to us in the future.

Our brains have evolved to express empathy and kindness in a certain way, a way that makes perfect sense from an evolutionary perspective. But when our goal is to improve the world as much as possible, rather than just to pass on our genes, those predispositions can mislead us. They can steer us away from the charitable decisions that would accomplish the most good.

Since that's the case, as odd as this may sound, we probably shouldn't base our charity decisions off of empathy. You and I feel empathy today because that feeling helped our ancestors survive in ages past. But that doesn't mean that following our empathetic impulses is a good way to do charity. In fact, as we've seen in this chapter, our empathy has glaring biases that can lead us to make inefficient charity decisions. It's only once we add in logic and reasoning that we can make the smart, calculated choices that do the most good.

Empathy is an extremely powerful force, and it is often the force that moves us to want to make the world a better place. We should let it move us. But we shouldn't let it dictate the direction we're moved in. Empathy should be the gas in our tank, but not the directions in our GPS. We need to, in essence, tell evolution: "Thanks for motivating me to care about others, but now I'm going to use that motivation for my own goal [making the world a better place] and not yours."

More Biases and Other Mental Quirks

The tendency to care more about those who are similar to us is not the only other bias that can steer us in the wrong direction when we're trying to do good.

Consider, for example, our bias to care more about individuals and less about groups of individuals. As former Soviet leader Josef Stalin is reported (probably incorrectly) to have said: "The death of one man is a tragedy, the death of millions is a statistic" (Wikiquote, 2014). While this may sound heinous coming from the mouth of a mass murderer, the psychological truth it hints at is a real one.

In one study, researchers at the University of Pennsylvania found that donors contributed more money to a hunger relief organization when they heard a story about one person who was starving than when they heard about millions of people who were starving. If our charitable decisions were logical, hearing that many people were starving should probably lead us to donate more. After all, it would mean there was a greater need for our help. But our mental hardwiring makes it easier for us to empathize with an individual than with an entire group. Plus, it seems hopeless to attempt to save large groups, whereas helping one individual feels like something we could accomplish.

Left unchecked, this bias can steer us toward some bad charity decisions, even beyond the decision to give less money when more individuals are in need. It can lead us to prefer making one child's wish come true to greatly improving the lives of dozens of other children. It can make donating to help one particular political prisoner appealing and donating to create systemic change that spares dozens of people from the same fate far less appealing.

Another bias that we all have is a bias toward preferring the status quo. In study after study, researchers have found that we tend to not want to change. We tend to think that the way things are now is better than possible alternatives. For example, in one study participants were told about two different policies a school district was choosing between. One was labeled the existing policy, and one was labeled as a potential new approach. Researchers found that, regardless of which policy was labeled as which, people tended to prefer the one that was labeled as the existing policy. They had a bias for the status quo. Other research has found that, when faced with lots of new options, we become paralyzed with indecision and even more likely to stick with what we've done in the past.

This makes a lot of sense from an evolutionary perspective. Why should we walk some unknown path through the woods, where a mountain lion could be lurking, when there's a safe path we've walked a hundred times before? When it comes to charity though, the tendency to stick with the status quo can lead us to continue donating to the same charity year after year without regard for how successful it has been. The *Money for Good* study found that, once people began donating to a particular charity, they were very unlikely to later switch to a different group. By and large, people kept writing checks to the same organization year in and year out. Such loyalty is great if the organization we're supporting is a really successful one. But it also means that we're unlikely to leave the mediocre charities we currently donate to for the great charities we don't yet donate to.

One last bias worth mentioning is what's called the "social norms bias." What social norms boil down to is pretty simple: when we see that lots of other people are doing something, we're more likely to do it. In one study, for example, a hotel found that the best way to get guests to re-use bath towels (instead of requesting fresh towels every day) was to put up small placards stating that most guests in the hotel re-use their towels.

Like our other biases, copying what other people are doing makes sense from an evolutionary perspective. If many other people are doing something, it's probably a safe and good thing to do. But when it comes to charity, this bias can lead us to donate to big brand-name charities without questioning how much positive impact they're having. Knowing that organizations like the Salvation Army, Red Cross, and United Way have lots of money and supporters can lead us to assume they are good places for us to donate to as well. We think that if everyone else is donating to them, there must be a good reason why. But that's not necessarily the case. How big and popular an organization is has almost no relationship to how effective it is at doing good. When it come to charity, our tendency to copy what others are doing can lead us in the wrong direction—a well-trod wrong direction, but a wrong direction nonetheless.

In addition to the biases we've just discussed, it's worth noting that we have lots of mental quirks that can also influence our charity decisions. For example, when we sign a petition for a cause we already support, we instantly become twice as likely to donate money to that cause—purely as a result of signing the petition. When we are given a small gift, we are more likely to make additional and larger donations to the organization that sent us the gift. Any of us who donate to charity have probably received these in the mail; some non-profits churn out notepads, address labels, blankets, bags, and other swag at an incredible rate.

Being told that "anything helps" also leads us to donate more. Seeing a credit card logo makes us more likely to donate. Certain headlines and images make us significantly more likely to pony up. Even certain colors make us more inclined to give. The list goes on.

While fairly harmless, these odd phenomena further highlight what our discussion of biases has already found. When we do good—whether as a donor, a volunteer, or a non-profit staffer—we are not in the driver's seat as much as we think we are. We are often being steered in large part by mental processes that we don't even know are going on.

Defeating Our Brains and Doing as Much Good as Possible

The view we have of our own charitable actions—as self-directed, logical, and compassionate choices to improve the world—is really just seeing the tip of the iceberg. The majority of what's driving our decisions operates below the surface. Only when we make a conscious effort to pay attention to our own biases and to base charitable decisions not on instinct but on the logical question of what will produce the most good in the world, can we—to some extent anyway—avoid the charity missteps that our brains drive us toward.

While the biases that evolution has carved into our brains are very real and very powerful, they should not be viewed as an excuse to short-change charity. Our instinctual bias to have more empathy for people of our own race than for people of other races is not an excuse to live in a racist manner. Similarly, the fact that we feel emotionally drawn toward certain charitable causes and organizations doesn't mean those are the ones we should support.

If we take charity seriously, then we need to be on the lookout against ourselves. If we want to succeed at the goal of charity—decreasing suffering and increasing well-being as much as possible—we need to be sure that logic and not bias is in the driver's seat. The good news is that the more aware we are of what our brains are trying to do to us, the more we can outsmart them and truly become great at doing good.

An easy way to do this is to always ask ourselves two questions when making a charity decision. First, "What's compelling me to want to take this action?" and second, "What similar action would do even more good?"

Imagine you receive a donation request letter from United Way that shows the face of a sad little girl in need of your support. Ask yourself, "What's compelling me to want to take action?" Notice that the story and picture were designed to pull your heartstrings. Realize that you feel more motivated to donate because you are hearing about one specific girl. Realize that because she lives in the United States, and perhaps even in your area, you are inclined to care more about her than a girl of the same age from another country. Realize that because you've heard of United Way before you are more trusting of them and probably more open to giving them money. Consider whether your instinct to donate to United Way right now is really based on a desire to help children in need, or whether it's more about you wanting to feel the warm glow of satisfaction from having done something good to help others.

Now, having realized all of these biases that are at play in your mind, stop and think logically about your decision. If you really care about children, then you want your donation to go to the organization and program that will help the greatest number of children. That means any children, because those in another state or country have just as much value as the little girl in the United Way letter. Are there other organizations and other programs that will do more good for more children with your donation than United Way will? If so, those are the organizations and programs you should donate toward. Last, is helping children even the cause you want to donate to? It may well be, but there are many individuals who suffer in many ways, not just children. Is your decision of where to donate based on what's going to do the most good, or are you just responding to a request that happened to arrive in your mailbox?

This is what overcoming bias looks like. While we'll never be perfect, the more attention we pay to our own biases, the more we'll be able to avoid being guided by them. That will leave us more free—free to make smarter, more rational choices about where to donate and what programs to carry out. We'll be free to make the world as much of a better place as possible without the weight of our mental biases dragging us down.

Putting Our Self-Centeredness to Work

Earlier in this chapter, we looked at how our inherent self-centeredness tries to steer us in the direction of doing what's best for us, even when carrying out charity work. In the last section we discussed how, once we're aware of that fact, we can overcome it and make more logical and effective charity decisions. But there's one more benefit to realizing just how many of our drives and mental reward systems are focused on ourselves: once we're aware of them, we can actually harness these self-centered tendencies and use them to help us succeed at charity.

The drive to excel at anything—be it basketball, business, or curing blindness—is fueled in large part by the desire for personal emotional gain. We want the feeling of pride and dominance that comes from competing and winning, from being the best at something, from improving on our own past performance. We want the thrill of defeating an enemy or obstacle. We want the satisfaction of solving challenges and the pleasure of attaining mastery over a skill.

There are reasons why entrepreneurs are willing to pour sixteen-hour workdays and their life savings into getting a new business off the ground. Because the business is born out of their own creative vision and their own hard work, its success or failure feels equivalent to their own success or failure as a person.

There are reasons why aspiring writers are willing to type late into the night for years on end in hopes of publishing the great American novel. For most people, there is a deeply satisfying pleasure in turning inner beliefs and feelings into a tangible creation that others can behold.

There are reasons why elite athletes are willing to push themselves to extreme lengths while training to compete. The feeling of triumph that comes from winning—be it a game, a championship, or an Olympic medal—can be euphoric. The feeling of failure can be devastating.

The deep-seated drive for personal emotional gain pushes people to work harder and achieve greater levels of success. We can use that same drive to push ourselves toward greater success at charity. If we define personal success, achievement, value, dominance, and creativity around the goal of charity—reducing suffering and increasing well-being as much as possible—than we can put our self-centered emotional reward system to good use.

Think back to earlier in the book when you were director of the Kalamazoo Rabbit Rescue Alliance. If your sense of personal and professional success was tied in with how many rabbits you rescued, you'd probably end up rescuing a lot more rabbits than if you were guided only by altruism. If your desire for self-improvement made you determined to have a lower cost per rabbit saved than you had the year before, you'd probably succeed in driving the cost down further than you would have otherwise. If you focused your creativity and the joy of creative expression on rabbit rescue, you'd probably come up with innovative ways to save even more rabbits.

When these personal emotional motivators aren't under control—when they use us, instead of us using them—they will sabotage our efforts. Anyone who works in the non-profit field has encountered organizations whose competitiveness makes them prioritize their own success and reputation over the good of the cause they purport to serve. Anyone who works in the non-profit field has probably also faced staffers whose insecurity, jealousy, or desire for status leads them to act like a jerk toward others. Such situations remind us that, while we can tap into personal emotional drives to push ourselves to work harder and smarter, those drives themselves should never be in control. But when these personal motivators are under our control, when we can see them inside ourselves and consciously harness them to work harder, smarter, and more creatively, our ability to make the world a better place will grow.

All of our strategic decisions, such as which issue to work on and which programs to carry out, should be made based on data. The cold logic of the bottom line should tell us where to steer the ship. But by defining our own personal success around the goal of charity, we can infuse the day-to-day work of manning the wheel with extra vigor. We can set up a personal reward system that makes us feel good to the extent we have improved the world.

In that way we can approach charity with the logic and rigor it deserves, carrying out the work that is most effective, and at the same time feel personally driven, rewarded, and satisfied.

8

THE ADVICE WE ARE GIVEN ABOUT CHARITY IS WRONG—HERE'S THE TRUTH

In your mind, picture the sort of person you think is likely to do charity work, whether as a staffer, donor, or volunteer.

Probably the person you're picturing is a bit more empathetic and kind than the average American. It may be someone who is a bit more sensitive, both to others' pain and also to their own. It's probably someone who wants to be a good, ethical person. It's someone who prefers collaboration and community over competitiveness and control. While personality traits like these might be helpful for leading us to do charity work, unfortunately, these same traits can prevent us from being as successful as possible at it.

Our empathy for others can make it difficult to take a dispassionate, calculated approach to doing good instead of simply responding to what's in front of us. Our desire to be good people can lead us to focus more on our intention to do good and less on exactly how much good we've accomplished. Our discomfort with hurting other people's feelings can dissuade us from critiquing the charity decisions of others. Our sensitivity can lead us to take critiques of our own work personally and can make it hard to admit to ourselves when we could be doing things a lot better. Our lack of competitiveness can make us less hungry to be the best in our fields or to conquer the social problems we're addressing.

These personality traits don't just color a few people's approaches to doing good. They strongly shape charity culture as a whole, influencing what we tell one another about how to go about doing good. But when we put the advice that comes standard in the charity world under a microscope—the advice that other people give us, and that we eventually start repeating ourselves—we see an odd pattern emerging. Much of the advice seeks to validate and benefit the individuals carrying out charity work, at the expense of those the charity work is supposed to help. It is great advice for those who want to feel good. It is terrible advice for those who want to do good.

The fact is that most of the standard-issue advice we've been told about how to do charity is flat out wrong. It sounds good, and it would work great for inspirational posters we could hang on our walls, but it's horrible advice to follow if we want to improve the world as much as possible.

In this chapter, we're going to reality-check some of that standard advice. Instead of trusting in feel-good maxims, we're going to put them under the microscope. Then we'll see what advice we should really take if we want to become great at doing good.

Following Your Passion Is a Bad Idea

We're often told that we should follow our passion and do what we love. That can be good advice in some situations. Consider a college student who's trying to decide what career he wants. Should he pursue a high-paying corporate lawyer position? Sure, he might have a starting salary of $120,000 a year, but he wouldn't have any free time and he'd be somewhat unhappy. Or should he pursue his dream of making glass sculptures? He wouldn't make very much money, but at least he'd be doing what he loved.

If living a relaxed life doing what he loved to do was this student's main priority, following his passion could be good advice to take. But maybe that isn't his main priority. Maybe he's a student from India who wants to earn as much money as possible so he can lift his extended family out of poverty. In that case, telling him to follow his passion would be bad advice. He should probably take the highest-paying job he can find. The point is that the approach the student should take depends a lot on what his goals are. For certain goals, following his passion would be a terrible way to try to reach them.

The same principle holds true when it comes to charity. If our main goal in doing charity work is to obtain personal enjoyment by supporting a good cause that interests us, then yes, following our passion could be a good idea. But if our main goal in doing charity work is to make the world a better place, then we should do the work that will accomplish the most good. Odds are that the charity work that will accomplish the most good is not the charity work that we initially feel most passionate about.

As with so much standard charity advice, the idea that we should follow our passion is a self-serving maxim that wraps itself in the cloak of altruism. What it really tells us is that our own enjoyment should come first and that we should follow that enjoyment where it takes us. How much we actually help the world is secondary in importance.

Wait, we might tell ourselves. Won't we be able to do the most good for the world if we're doing what we're passionate about? That feels like it might be true, and it would be a great win-win situation if it were. But it usually isn't.

Are we likely to perform better at a particular task if we're passionate about it? Of course. But even if that passion led us to perform two, three, or even ten times better, it would still be no match for the massive range in impact that exists between different fields of charity.

Consider Kevin. Kevin is more passionate about the theater than any other person in New York City. He lives and breathes it. Not only that, but he has an incredible knack for exciting others about attending the theater. On the other hand, Kevin cares nothing about blind people. He's never thought about them a day in his life.

When choosing how to volunteer his time, should Kevin volunteer for the Theatre Communications Group or the Seva Foundation? Following his passion would obviously mean volunteering for TCG, and some people might encourage him to do just that.

But the fact is that Kevin would do far more good for the world by volunteering with Seva. Even if his free volunteer labor helps Seva save a mere $200 in extra expenses, that money saved would have a big impact: several additional people would be spared from blindness. That would be a far greater good than Kevin could accomplish at TCG, no matter how stellar a volunteer he was for the group. Even if his passion led thousands of additional people to visit and enjoy the theater, that would still be (to most of us) a far smaller good than curing several people of blindness.

It's true that passion and effectiveness sometimes overlap. Some people who make lots of money are passionate about their jobs. Some people who accomplish a ton of good in the non-profit sector are passionate about the issue they're involved with. But when deciding what type of charity work we should do—as a donor, volunteer, or non-profit staffer—passion should not be our guide. The goal of charity is to make the world a better place, so our charity decisions should be based on what will best achieve that. If passion eventually follows, great—that is icing on the cake. If it doesn't, that's what hobbies are for. We can do what we're most passionate about in our spare time and have our charity work remain focused on whatever will help the world as much as possible.

The good news is that, for many of us, we'll eventually become passionate about whatever type of charity work we choose to do, even if we don't feel that way at the start. When we become deeply involved with something positive, we tend to become enthusiastic about it. Knowing how much good our charity work is doing for the world makes it all the more likely that, when we lead with our brains, our hearts will follow.

Being Great at What You Do Doesn't Matter Unless You're Doing the Right Thing

Earlier we referenced author Jim Collins and his business classic *Good to Great*, which explores why some companies become great and others remain merely good. The key metric Collins and his research team used to identify great companies was stock performance. Companies that had a period of fifteen or more years where their stock price followed the industry average, followed by a period of fifteen or more years where their stock price dramatically outpaced the industry average, were deemed great companies. While not everyone would agree that stock price is what matters most, Collins and company deserve credit for defining a specific and meaningful metric on which to assess the greatness of a business.

Years after *Good to Great* came out, Collins published a small monograph entitled *Good to Great and the Social Sectors*. In it, he tries to apply his *Good to Great* principles to organizations in non-profit or government fields. But while Collins has a well-defined metric for identifying greatness in the for-profit sector, his metric for identifying greatness among charities was as fuzzy as could be.

Great charities, Collins says, are those that excel at what they do and that become leaders in their own fields. He presents the Cleveland Symphony Orchestra as an example of a charity that has achieved greatness. Collins describes how, under the direction of a new conductor, the Cleveland Symphony began packing houses, being invited to perform at prestigious events, and having its style imitated by other orchestras around the country. From that, Collins concludes that it should be viewed as a great charity (Collins, 2005).

Does it appear the Cleveland Symphony Orchestra has achieved great success at creating beautiful music? Yes. Does it appear the Cleveland Symphony Orchestra has had great success at achieving the goal of charity? No. When it comes to achieving the goal of charity—making the world a better place—the orchestra will never be anywhere remotely close to the top of the charity pack. It won't ever come close to doing as much good for the world as smaller, less prestigious charities that are working on more high-impact causes. For non-profit organizations, being great at what you do is far less important than choosing the right thing to do.

The same holds true for individual volunteers and staffers. Think back to Kevin, the theater enthusiast. What I didn't tell you before is that not only does Kevin love the theater passionately, but he is also a trained and experienced communications professional. In fact, he excels at facilitating communication. Just last year the New York City Communications Professionals Association presented him with their "Communicator of the Year" award. On the other hand, Kevin is terrible at stuffing envelopes. He is slow, his fingers aren't nimble, and it takes him forever to seal the envelopes correctly.

Kevin has decided to spend more time volunteering and, as before, he's trying to decide whether to volunteer for the Theatre Communications Group or the Seva Foundation. If he volunteers for TCG, he will help them with their communications work—something he is literally the best in the city at. If he volunteers for Seva, he will help them stuff envelopes to mail to donors—something he is pretty bad at. Which should Kevin choose?

Standard charity advice would tell him to do what he's good at. Clearly, that would mean volunteering for the Theatre Communications Group. Yet volunteering for Seva would accomplish more good than volunteering for TCG, in spite of the fact that Kevin is great at communicating and terrible at stuffing envelopes. Even if Kevin's slow, fumbling work eventually helped Seva raise a few hundred extra dollars, several more people would be spared from blindness. That is a greater amount of good than Kevin could accomplish with even an incredible volunteer performance at TCG.

(The only thing Kevin would need to make sure of was that he was not taking the place of another, more efficient volunteer. If Seva had a volunteer who was great at stuffing envelopes, but who couldn't volunteer because Kevin was in his seat, Kevin would do more harm than good. If that were the case though, Seva's volunteer manager would probably realize it and politely ask Kevin to come at a different time.)

The point is that being great at what you do doesn't matter much unless you're doing the right thing. In fact, if you're not doing the right thing, being great at what you do could actually be harmful.

Consider Kevin's wife Rachel, who happens to be the single greatest fundraising professional who has ever walked the face of the earth. Her charm, intelligence, and persuasiveness are incredibly effective at persuading people to give money when she asks for it. While Rachel should be proud of her skills, she should realize they have as much ability to do harm as to do good.

Imagine that Rachel is the director of development for the Theatre Communications Group. Thanks to her great skill, she's able to double the group's income from $10 million to $20 million in a single year. While that sounds great, because TCG is a relatively low-impact charity, this increase in budget doesn't improve the world all that much. Meanwhile, the fact that more money is going toward TCG means the public will probably donate less to other, more effective charities—not necessarily $10 million less, but probably still somewhat less than they would have otherwise. Because of that, despite being the most talented fundraising professional alive, Rachel's overall impact on the world might actually have been a negative one. There may be more children who suffer from debilitating diseases, more people who remain blind, and so forth—all because of how great Rachel was at bringing more donor dollars to the field of theater communications.

Once again, when it comes to succeeding at charity, what you do is much more important than whether or not you are great at what you're doing. Just as the question "What am I passionate about?" should not guide our charity decisions, the question "What am I good at?" should not guide our decisions either. Instead, the key question we should ask ourselves is this: "What can I do that will produce the most good?"

Sometimes what will produce the most good is something we are good at. But often the path that will do the most good is not something we are uniquely skilled at it—at least not at the start.

Not All Charity Work Is Needed or Worth Doing Right Now

When faced with the hard fact that certain types of charity work do far more good than others, a common justification for continuing to support less-effective work is the idea that "it's all needed." Someone needs to plant gardens. Someone needs to teach after-school programs. Someone needs to clean rivers. Someone needs to feed the homeless. Someone needs to produce art that enriches our lives. Someone needs to feed the hungry. Someone needs to advocate for marriage equality. Because all of these things are needed, they are all worth doing.

In a world that had infinite money and infinite time that could go toward making the world a better place, then yes it wouldn't really matter which type of charity work we decided to do. Because everything was going to be done, it wouldn't really matter which piece of the puzzle we personally chose to work on.

But that's not the world we live in. Each of us has a very limited amount of time, money, and energy to devote to charity. While every type of charity work is valuable, the idea that "it's all needed" implies that there's no need to prioritize certain types of work over others. But do we really believe that?

Imagine that the American Civil War is raging and you are the Union Army's chief medic. The Battle of Gettysburg has just ended and the Confederate Army is in retreat. The dead, dying, injured, and fatigued lie strewn for miles across the battlefield. Your medical staff, meanwhile, consists of just four ill-equipped doctors. Primitive medical supplies in hand, you rush in to begin tending to the wounded.

The first soldier you come to has had the lower portion of his leg blown off by a cannonball. The stump is bleeding profusely, and he's in definite danger of dying if the wound isn't closed soon. You immediately set to work cleaning it, bandaging it, applying a tourniquet to stop the bleeding, and providing some whisky to the soldier to help him deal with the pain.

Twenty minutes later, the job is done. The soldier has been treated, and if all goes well he'll live. Quickly you rise and hurry to find the next person in need of treatment. A few paces on you come to a soldier with a broken pinkie finger. He's not in that much pain, and his injury is not life-threatening, so you continue past him without stopping.

Twenty feet further, you come across a soldier who is not injured at all, just in shock and dehydrated. You pass him a flask of water then hurry on. A few feet past him, you find a soldier with a bullet hole in his lower chest. He's going to need immediate surgery to remove the bullet and stop the bleeding, otherwise he'll be dead within hours. You immediately take his shirt off and begin to work.

As you do, out of the corner of your eye you notice one of your medical staffers. He is squatting by the soldier with the broken pinkie, gently wrapping a splint and bandage around the swollen finger. He provides whisky to the soldier to help him deal with the pain and a shoulder to cry on as the soldier sits weeping over losing his brother in the battle.

As chief medic, what do you do? Do you shout at the medical staffer that men are dying out here and that he needs to treat soldiers with life-threatening wounds before worrying about broken pinkies and tear-stained faces? Or do you tell him to keep up the good work, because there are all sorts of problems on the battlefield and every type of help is needed?

Like medics on the battlefield, those of us doing charity work are in a triage situation. All sorts of problems could be and ideally should be addressed. But if we are truly compassionate, we will focus on the worst and most treatable issues first. Once millions of people are not suffering each day from easily reversible blindness, we can worry about theater communication. Once critical portions of the ecosystem are not collapsing from overpopulation and resource overuse, we can worry about supporting our alma mater. That doesn't mean we have to stamp out every single case of blindness and every single instance of environmental degradation before donating a penny to less efficient charities. Rather, it means that at any given time we should do the work that is going to most benefit the world. Usually, this means focusing on the worst and most treatable issues.

To add a bit of nuance here, we should note the important difference between doing a *type* of work that is incredibly important and doing the work where *we personally* will have the biggest impact. For example, education is important for a whole host of reasons. If people don't have the ability to read, write, think critically, and understand the world enough to make compassionate decisions, very few problems are going to be solved. Hospitals are also very important; they keep us healthy, they ease our pain when we're in agony, and they can save lives. But when deciding where to donate, volunteer, or do non-profit work, the question to ask is not, "Is this type of work extremely important," but rather, "What difference will come about in the world if I personally do this?"

Education organizations and hospitals are incredibly important and should be funded, and they are, to the tune of many billions of dollars. How much additional good would actually be brought about in the world if we give them an additional $1,000? Probably not much. Probably a lot less good than if we donated that $1,000 to organizations like Seva or Mercy for Animals, which would actually reduce several cases of blindness or spare hundreds of animals from a lifetime of suffering with that money.

Sure, teachers can change lives and doctors can save lives. But how much additional good would actually be brought about in the world if we personally took one of those jobs? They are paid positions, so if we don't do the work someone else will. There are already hundreds of thousands if not millions of very intelligent, very passionate, very capable people who want to be teachers and doctors. The number of very intelligent, very passionate, and very capable people who want to work at highly efficient non-profits is miniscule. Our skills are much more needed there—and will probably go much further there.

Part of the reason it's hard to prioritize where we should donate and what we should do is our distance from the problems of the world. On the battlefield every one of us would have tended to the most seriously wounded before moving on to the less seriously wounded. We would have done so, even if it meant many of the less seriously wounded didn't receive any treatment at all. But today, most of us in the Western world are rarely face-to-face with the worst types of suffering that charity seeks to alleviate. We know they exist, but because they're not visible right in front of us they don't have a lot of emotional resonance. Instead, the problems of the world melt into a general stew. Focusing on any one issue feels just as important as focusing on any other. But it's not.

If we lived in a malnutrition-ravaged region of Somalia, and we had the choice between having additional rice and vegetables for our children or having murals painted on the walls of our tin shacks, which would we want? What would we say to relief workers from the United States who drove into town with paint buckets and brushes instead of food? Believing that all charity work is equally important is like patting the backs of those relief workers who arrived with paint buckets and no food and telling them, "Good work! Sure our children's bellies will continue to be swollen and their growth will continue to be stunted, but at least we'll have pretty buildings to look at."

In 2013, Americans gave $14.4 billion to arts and culture organizations. This is more than half the amount given to support public health. It's close to double the amount spent on protecting the environment and animals combined, even though we live in an era when environmental destruction and animal cruelty are occurring on scales unprecedented in human history. In 2013,

Americans also gave $34 billion in donations to colleges and universities, all of which went on top of the money these schools already brought in from exorbitantly high student tuitions. If just a portion of those donating to the arts or to universities decided to put their money toward more urgent causes instead, imagine how much good could be done. Preventable blindness could be completely eradicated throughout the world. Schistosomiasis could be completely treated, sparing 200 million people a year. Hundreds of millions of animals could be spared from a lifetime of terrible misery. Major inroads could be made toward protecting the health of the planet's ecosystems.

These are just a few examples of what the world will stand to gain when, like the battlefield medic, we as a charitable people prioritize more urgent issues over less urgent ones. For now, all of these terrible tragedies continue on unnecessarily. That is the incredible price the world pays for our failure to prioritize when doing good.

The idea that "it's all needed," and that therefore all charitable work is equally worth doing, is a dangerous one. As with "follow your passion," it is a self-serving idea that wraps itself in the cloak of altruism. It provides a justification for continuing to do exactly what we're doing now and for working on whatever issue we enjoy working on, even when supporting another cause would accomplish far more good.

It also gives us an excuse for not questioning the charity work of others. When someone else could be accomplishing much more with his or her time, money, and energy, the idea that "it's all needed" gives us a reason to refrain from raising that impolite fact. It allows us to avoid the mild displeasure of pointing out something that is important but that may hurt someone's feelings. Instead, we can extend a friendly pat on the back and say, "Keep doing what you're doing; it's all needed." They feel good. We feel good. It's only those individuals who are suffering just outside our sights who pay the price.

We Have to Make Hard Decisions About Who to Help and Who to Ignore

Ngan's parents were poor rice farmers, struggling to survive. When they saw her cleft lip and cleft palate for the first time, they thought she'd been cursed. Neighbors pitied her. Other children were afraid to look at her. Generous friends like you enabled us to give Ngan the surgery she needed—and save her from shame and rejection. She now has a terrific smile and a bright future ahead. Such a transformation seems miraculous! But we cannot rest. We want to go to more places and help more children [Fritz, 2014].

—Operation Smile fundraising appeal

Anecdotes are the bread and butter of non-profit fundraising appeals. Whether it's the story of a young child healed of a cleft palate by Operation Smile, a struggling family that has a home thanks to Habitat for Humanity, or a survivor pulled from the wreckage of a disaster by the Red Cross, stories humanize the work that non-profits do and inspire the public to act, to donate, and to volunteer. Using anecdotes and focusing on individuals therefore makes a lot of sense when communicating the organization's work to the public.

Internally though, decisions on what programs to run and how to run them should be based around a non-profit's bottom line. That means that if we want to improve the world as much as possible, we must make calculated decisions about who to help and who to refrain from helping.

Imagine that you're a program director for the Seva Foundation, and your goal is to cure as many people as possible from blindness in the regions of Nepal and Vietnam. Right now, there are far more people who need treatment in these countries than you have the funds to treat. Since you are the only organization doing this sort of work in these countries, that means that tens of thousands of people in each region will remain blind when they could be cured.

After a year on the job, you realize that the cost of curing a person of blindness in Nepal is cheaper than the cost of curing someone in Vietnam. You do some calculations and realize that your cost per person cured in Nepal is $50, and the cost per person cured in Vietnam is $70. When deciding where to allocate funds next year, which country should you focus your spending on? Just Nepal? Just Vietnam? Should you continue to operate in both countries?

If you focused your funding just on Nepal, your overall cost per person cured of blindness would probably go down and you'd be able to help far more people. For example, if your total budget between the two countries was $300,000 a year, you'd be able to cure about 1,700 extra people a year of blindness by directing all of your funding to Nepal. But that would mean turning your back on the people of Vietnam. It would mean that people suffering from easily reversible blindness in that country would have no one to help them, simply because—through no fault of their own—the cost of operating there was slightly higher than it was in a neighboring country.

Would that be fair to people in Vietnam? Not at all. Would it feel good to shut down operations there and abandon those Vietnamese in need? Certainly not. But if our goal is to cure as many people as possible from blindness, the unpleasant fact is that an approach of only operating in Nepal would mean curing more people. It definitely isn't fair to blind people in Vietnam to ignore them because they cost more to treat. But it would be unfair to people overall if we acted in a way that reduced the total number of individuals we could cure from blindness.

Similarly, medical relief organizations like Doctors Without Borders must decide whom they will treat and what types of care they will provide. Should they focus on treating only a few key illnesses that are common, life-threatening, and easily curable? If so, their clinics would have to turn away patients with less common illnesses as well as patients with illnesses that are more expensive to treat. Should Doctors Without Borders decide instead to treat all patients who come to them, regardless of the illness? Since resources are limited, that approach would mean many people with life-threatening but easily curable illnesses would be left to die, and people with minor illnesses would take their place in clinic waiting rooms.

Should environmental organizations focus on promoting family planning in the United States and around the globe in order to decrease overpopulation and the strain it puts on the environment? Or should they focus on stopping specific old growth forests from being cut down now or stopping a certain new coal-fired power plant from being built? Decreasing overpopulation would probably do much more good for the environment in the long run, but that would mean ignoring environmental harms that are being done right now.

Donors face similar questions. When donating to fight malnutrition, should we support organizations working in America or organizations working in Africa, India, and elsewhere around the world? Malnutrition in the United States is—while a real problem—not nearly as extreme as malnutrition in many other countries. It's also much cheaper to prevent malnutrition in developing countries like India than it is in the United States. But donating to help those who are suffering overseas requires refraining from donating to help those who share our streets, schools, and subways.

Saying that we can "do both" does not enable us to avoid these tough decisions. As long as there are more individuals to help than our resources allow us to, charity is a zero-sum game. Because each of us has limited time and money, choosing to do one thing means choosing to not do something else. Choosing to support less effective charity work means more individuals will suffer than if we had stuck with supporting only the most effective work. That remains true no matter how much money we have already given to very effective charity work. Even if you as a Seva manager are already spending 90 percent of your funding on Nepal, it is still the case that you can cure more people of blindness by moving the remaining 10 percent to Nepal as well.

Standard charity advice tells us to help anyone we can, to help whomever is in need in front of us. But the reality is that, if we really want to succeed at doing good, we need to make calculated rather than indiscriminate decisions about which individuals to help. Improving the world as much as possible sometimes requires that we refrain from helping those who are suffering in front of us so that we remain able to help those who are suffering out of sight.

Taking that approach demands a rigorous type of caring, one that runs counter to our instincts and counter to our common-sense understanding of what it means to do good. But if our goal really is to improve the world as much as possible, it is the approach that will enable us to succeed.

Doing Good Doesn't Always Feel Good

As we just saw, if we want to do as much good as we can for the world, we must translate living, breathing individuals into numbers when we're making charity decisions. Doing that doesn't feel very good. If anything, it feels a little inhuman. It also doesn't feel very compassionate to turn away from individuals in need who are right in front of us.

All of which seems to contradict something else we've been told about charity: that we will feel good when we do good. We are taught that helping others should leave us with the warm glow of satisfaction that makes doing good its own reward. So why is it that the charity decisions that accomplish the most good don't always give us a nice fuzzy feeling?

Most of us feel revulsion at the idea of turning individuals into numbers, and rightfully so. It's de-individualization that leads to so many problems and cruelties in the first place. It's easier to disregard poverty, support a new war, eat meat, and so forth when we can avoid seeing those who are suffering as specific individuals.

When we meet someone in poverty and hear about her struggles, it becomes harder to ignore the problem she is going through. When we meet a specific pig and spend time with her, it becomes harder to ignore the terrible suffering she or others like her go through when they are raised and killed to be eaten. So when it comes to persuading others to care about an issue, and when it comes to developing our own ethical beliefs, we should look at individuals as just that—unique individuals with their own inherent value.

That's why translating individuals into numbers when we're doing charity work seems so counterintuitive and so, well, wrong. Think back to our example from the last section. Making a calculated decision to stop treating blindness in Vietnam, and move all of that funding to Nepal instead, may seem a bit cold and heartless. A policy of treating all blind people who need help, regardless of the particular cost each patient has, seems much more compassionate. In fact, if we were running that program at Seva, we may view a policy of operating in both countries despite the cost difference as a badge of honor: we are so compassionate that we don't turn away any person unless we're completely out of funds. (A policy of continuing to treat people in both countries would also work better for us as a program director; it would prevent us from feeling a rush of guilt that might come from abandoning an entire population that we had previously been helping.)

But when we look to the real-world results, we see the exact opposite is true. If we disregard the reality that some people are cheaper to treat than others, we are condemning a greater number of people to suffer from reversible blindness. The approach that *feels* heartlessly calculating would actually help many more people—and result in far more people being spared from blindness.

We should say that again, because it bears repeating: when it comes to making charity decisions, an approach that feels cold and heartless—counting individuals as numbers—can actually produce the most compassionate results. Succeeding at charity, then, requires a deeper, more challenging type of compassion—one focused on end results and not on how things feel in the moment.

The idea that we as Seva's program director might be inclined to embrace is a common one in the charity world: never turn away from an individual in need if you can help him or her. But like so much of the advice we have been told about how to do charity, this is a self-serving idea that wraps itself in the cloak of altruism. Because we do not want to feel the guilt of turning someone away or because we lack the self-discipline to do so, we provide care to those who are in front of us at the expense of the many who are not. In a grimly ironic twist, we view the truly charitable decision, the one that achieves the most good in the world, as callous and wrong simply because it *feels* that way.

The fact is that it doesn't always feel good to do good. Sometimes it feels bad to do the right thing. And sometimes, doing good doesn't feel like anything at all. Sometimes it can feel stunningly neutral and uneventful to us, as if nothing at all has happened—even when what we've done has dramatically impacted the lives of so many others.

And that's okay. As we all agreed at the start of the book, the goal of charity is not to benefit ourselves. It's not to feel good. So we should base our charity decisions not on what will feel good, but on what will do the most good—even if that makes us feel bad at times, and even if it sometimes makes us feel nothing at all.

Charity Is All About Winning

Most of us who do charity work really do want to make the world a better place. But, as we discussed in an earlier chapter, we also have personal motivations for doing good. We may be drawn to charity work because it allows us to express our beliefs and allows us to shape the world in the way we want to shape it. We may do it because it helps us feel good about ourselves for making a difference. It may add a greater sense of meaning and purpose to our lives.

While it's great that these personal motivations can lead us to do good for others, there is a downside: they can sometimes lead us to view doing good through the lens of ourselves. Specifically, they can lead us to think that the point of charity is "doing something good," a viewpoint fixed squarely on ourselves and our own actions. Did we "do good" or not? Contrast that with the actual goal of charity: to improve the world as much as possible. Here the focus is not on you or me, but on the rest of the world. How much did the world change? How much suffering was reduced, and how much well-being was increased? The fact that we "did good" isn't important; all that matters is what result we brought about.

When our personal motivations are in the driver's seat, we tend to see results as secondary in importance. The advice we've all been told about charity certainly reinforces that idea. We are told that we should give back, play our part, do good, donate to charity, be generous, and so forth. That sounds great, but all of these directives are focused on *us* and what *we* do, not on what happens in the world after we do those things. It's far less often that we're encouraged to bring about some specific change in the world like preventing hunger, curing blindness, or reducing overpopulation.

As a result, what is communicated to us is that charity is not about winning, but it's about doing good. Like a six-year-old heading onto the field for our first Little League game, we're told that it doesn't matter whether we win or lose, all that matters is that we give it our best shot. We're winners just for taking part. So when we donate or volunteer, we immediately feel like we're good people and that we've done our part. What happens after we drop our check in the mail or after we go home for the day is not something we pay particularly close attention to.

If we take charity seriously though, we must recognize that charity is all about winning. In fact, winning is the only thing that matters. We either reduce suffering or we don't. A man in rural India either stays blind for the rest of his life or he regains his sight. A young woman either contracts a debilitating disease or she doesn't. A hungry child either eats or stays hungry. Our intentions and beliefs don't matter. How much we sacrifice and how hard we work don't matter. Our goodness as individuals doesn't matter. All that matters is whether, and how much, we succeed at making the world a better place.

At the end of the day, charity is about one thing and one thing only: winning positive change. As football coach Vince Lombardi once said, "Winning isn't everything; it's the only thing" (Wikipedia, 2014). The more that we as donors, volunteers, and non-profit staffers adopt that mindset, the more quickly the world will become a better place.

9

MOVING FORWARD WITH HUMILITY

Admitting What We Don't Know

As we know, there are known knowns; there are
things that we know that we know. We also know
there are known unknowns; that is to say we know
there are some things we do not know. But there are
also unknown unknowns, the ones we don't know
we don't know. And if one looks throughout the
history of our country and other free countries, it is
the latter category that tend to be the difficult ones.
—*Donald Rumsfeld, former Secretary of Defense,*
U.S. Department of Defense, 2002.

Knowing What We Don't Know

In February of 2002, then-Secretary of Defense Donald Rumsfeld issued the above quote in response to a reporter's question on whether or not Iraq was supplying weapons of mass destruction to terrorist groups. While Rumsfeld's tongue-twister made him the butt of late-night talk show jokes, the sentiment he expressed has some real wisdom to it. The fact is there's an awful lot we don't know. Furthermore, our biggest problems occur when we don't even know that we don't know it.

If you drive a car, chances are that at least once in your life you've ended up pulled over on the side of the highway in the breakdown lane. Maybe there was smoke coming from under the hood. Maybe there was a really terrible noise that made clear

was seriously wrong. In any case, one thing was cer-
d a problem that needed to be fixed.

So you reached for your cell phone or walked to the nearest
pay phone to call a tow truck, then waited impatiently for the
truck to arrive, frustrated at having your day disrupted and thinking about all the things that could be wrong with the car and how
much it would cost to fix them. Finally, the tow truck showed up,
hooked your car up onto its bed, and as you climbed into the front
cab the driver turned and asked: "Where to?"

For most of us, the answer was that we wanted the car towed
to a repair shop. Why didn't we just ask to be towed back home or
onward to wherever we'd been driving? Because we had no idea
how to fix our car. It wasn't just that we lacked the right tools or
that we didn't have enough time. It's that we had no idea how to
solve the problem.

How to fix our car was, in the words of Rumsfeld, a "known
unknown." We knew that we didn't have a clue of how to fix the
problem and that we had to call on the help of someone who did.
Recognizing our own lack of knowledge was important. Just imagine how much time we would have wasted, and how much more
damage we could have done, if we foolishly assumed we knew how
to fix our broke-down car.

When faced with a smoking car that refuses to start, it's pretty
easy to admit that we don't know how to solve the problem. For
one thing, the reality will be obvious. Either the car starts or it
does not. We can't pretend we've fixed it when we haven't. Second, it's in our best interest to be honest. Trying to fix it ourselves
when we don't know how would just waste our time, and perhaps
even cost us money if we made things worse.

Unfortunately, we're not always so honest with ourselves and
others. Just ask Amanda Waterman.

Waterman is a developmental psychologist at the University
of Leeds whose research has centered on the question of why we're
so reluctant to admit when we don't know the answer to something. In one study, Waterman asked children questions for which

there was no real answer—for example, "Is red heavier than yellow?" or "Is a sweater angrier than a tree?" Although these are, of course, nonsensical questions, rather than answer "I don't know," many children asserted that they knew the answer. Yes, red was heavier than yellow. No, a sweater was not angrier than a tree (Freakonomics, 2014).

In another study, Waterman read children a very short story about a family's trip to the beach. She then asked them questions about the story that they could not know the answers to because the information hadn't been provided. For example, did the family drink lemonade? Did they listen to music in the car? There was no way the children could know because the story hadn't told them. Yet nearly three-quarters of the children gave a yes or no answer to these questions, even after Waterman repeatedly assured them they could say "I don't know."

While the adults in Waterman's studies were more honest about what they didn't know, a full 25 percent of them still claimed to know the answers, even when there was no way they could have, and even when they were reassured they could answer "I don't know." Her studies highlight something that all of us know from our own experience: we often pretend to know things when all we're really doing is taking a guess.

Why are we so hesitant to admit the limitations of our knowledge? Part of it probably comes down to pride. We want to know it all, to have all the answers. The smarter we appear to be, the prouder we will feel about ourselves and the more we think others will look up to us and respect us. Because knowing things has real value, knowledge can also be power. By appearing to know it all, we may be able to work ourselves into positions of increasing power and authority.

Perhaps the unwillingness to admit what we don't know is also due in part to our education system, which is primarily concerned with how much information has been absorbed. Every pop quiz, exam, and assignment is designed to measure one thing: how much you know. When you don't know the answer to a test question, what's the best thing to do? Take a guess. After all, there's a chance you'll be right. Since you'll end up being right some of the time, guessing—pretending that you know the answer—is always a better strategy than leaving the answer blank.

For seventeen formative years, students are consistently rewarded for pretending they know the answers. They are never rewarded for having the discernment to recognize when they don't know an answer. Imagine how different grading would look, and what a different mindset would be instilled in students, if that sort of discernment were encouraged and rewarded as part of the grading process.

Our need to appear to know it all does not end after we graduate from high school and college; it carries over into the working world as well. One piece of advice repeatedly given to job seekers is to never say "I don't know" during a job interview. From online publisher *Business Insider* to job posting site Monster.com, job seekers are repeatedly encouraged to never say those three deadly words for fear of looking unintelligent or unprepared. That mentality often remains even after the interview, with employees at all levels and in all fields reluctant to admit that there are many questions they can't answer.

This is obviously problematic. If we want to repair that car and get it driving smoothly again, we have to be very up-front with the fact that we don't know how to fix it. If we want to do a job right, whether on a car, at our workplace, or anywhere else, we have to be honest with ourselves and others about the limits of our knowledge.

What is also problematic is when we don't even know that we don't know. These are, to again quote from Rumsfeld, the "unknowns unknowns." Just what do we mean by that?

In his 2003 book *Moneyball: The Art of Winning an Unfair Game*, journalist Michael Lewis profiled Oakland Athletics manager Billy Beane and Beane's use of statistical analysis to build a better baseball team. For two decades, the Oakland A's had been one of the worst-funded teams in baseball. They had dramatically less money available to spend on players' salaries than other teams had, which made it difficult for the A's to recruit top-notch players. The team just couldn't afford them (Lewis, 2003).

Because he knew his team would always be outspent, Beane saw only one route to making his team one of the best in the major leagues: making smarter decisions about which players to hire. Rather than rely on the conventional wisdom of baseball insiders in deciding which players to bring on board, Beane and his team turned instead to statistical analysis. What they found was that the things most coaches and scouts looked to in determining how valuable a player was, things like batting average and whether a player seemed to have all-around skills, were not the best indicators of how much good a player would do for a team. Instead, the A's found certain data points that were much better at predicting how valuable a player would be—for example, on-base percentage and slugging percentage. (If these terms mean nothing to you, don't worry; we're done with the baseball jargon.)

With that data in hand, the A's were able to identify and hire players who both scored highly in those key areas and who were willing to accept a low salary because they weren't seen as particularly valuable by other teams. The approach worked. While the A's have yet to win a World Series under Beane, they've won their division five times in the past fifteen years—an impressive feat for any team, let alone one that is badly outspent by most of its competitors. In the wake of Oakland's success, a number of other baseball teams have adopted a similar approach to vetting and hiring new players.

Baseball is not a new game. Professional teams had existed in the United States for more than 125 years before Beane took the helm of the Oakland A's. Yet in all those years, no other manager or team had examined the data to see what best predicted a player's success. In a sense, this data was the "unknown unknown." Other baseball teams weren't pretending to know what the data said, like schoolchildren asserting that red is heavier than yellow. Rather, they didn't even know they should be looking at that data to determine which players to acquire. Because they didn't know they should be looking at it, they never took the time to crunch the numbers and learn what they could.

There are two key points here. First, we really hate saying, "I don't know," so we'll often take a guess and just pretend we know. Second, no matter how smart or experienced we are, there's always something that we're missing. And we don't even realize we should be looking for it.

The Wonderful World of Science

Over two thousand years ago in ancient Egypt, the practice we now call alchemy first began. Part philosophy, part magic, and part proto-science, alchemists pursued such noble goals as turning lead into gold and developing a potion that would confer eternal youth on those who drank it.

While we can look back today and laugh at the naïveté of those goals, in its time alchemy was taken very seriously. There were schools that taught alchemy, there were alchemy textbooks, and in certain countries governments issued licenses to professional alchemists. In fact, alchemy lasted about two millennia, until the 1700s and 1800s, at which point it was replaced by chemistry. (You may have noticed that the names have something in common.) But whereas alchemy produced almost nothing of direct value for humankind in its two-thousand-year history, in just a few short centuries chemistry has been wildly successful at improving and extending human life. If you enjoy modern medicine, your smart phone, or having clean drinking water come out of your faucet each morning, you can thank chemistry (in part) for each of those things.

So what was the difference between chemistry and alchemy? Why did one succeed so brilliantly while the other failed so miserably? The difference between the two was both simple and fundamental. Alchemists did not use the scientific method. Chemists did use, and do use, the scientific method.

At the heart of the scientific method is a simple but profound concept: if you're going to assert that something is true, you'd better have the testing to back it up. Testing is the heart of science. Look the word "science" up on Wikipedia and the first sentence will tell you that science builds and organizes knowledge in the form of testable explanations and predictions. Testing allowed chemists to prove and disprove certain things and thereby progress step-by-step out of the murky world of alchemy. Testing allows any knowledge-based discipline to advance to greater understanding and effectiveness.

It's no surprise to most of us that hard sciences like chemistry, physics, or biology advance as a result of testing. But those aren't the only areas of society in which testing is being used.

In the business world, every major corporation worth its salt uses testing and data to guide its decisions. These decisions include which features people like and want in a product, which target audiences should be advertised to, and which products or services to sell in the first place. Companies spend billions each year on market research for the simple fact that it helps them make more money.

In politics, testing is also now being used to win elections. In 2012 Barak Obama was re-elected President of the United States. While there are many reasons historians could point to in trying to understand why he won re-election, *The Los Angeles Times* and other publications singled out one factor as the secret weapon in Obama's arsenal: data.

The Obama campaign hired a team of more than fifty data analysts to amass a mountain of data on voters in swing states. Working out of a set of rooms in Chicago dubbed "The Cave," this team collected up to eighty pieces of data on these voters, everything from their age, gender, and religion to what magazines they subscribed to, how much their houses were worth, and so forth.

After all the data were collected, the Obama team ran tests to determine which demographic groups were most likely to be undecided voters who could be persuaded to vote for Obama. Further testing—carried out through countless phone calls, mailings, and door-to-door visits—showed which messages would be most effective at persuading undecided voters to lean toward Obama.

After the testing was done, the outreach effort was kicked into high gear. Hundreds of thousands of undecided voters in swing states were targeted at the individual level through mailings, door knocks, and telephone calls. They were targeted with scripts and materials specifically tailored to their demographic groups. The rest, as they say, is history. Obama won nearly every swing state and cruised to re-election.

Learning How to Do Good Instead of Guessing How to Do Good

Scientists, businesses executives, and political campaigners aren't the only ones who can turn to testing and data to become more effective at reaching their goals. Those of us who want to make the world a better place can do so, too.

Most charitable efforts are designed to address some problem: reduce poverty, prevent domestic abuse, end environmental destruction, stop human trafficking, and so forth. Some of the problems that charity tries to solve are relatively simple to understand and address. Others are torturously complex. The challenge for every person and every organization that wants to do good is figuring out the best, most effective way to help solve the problem. That is where our unwillingness to admit what we don't know can pose a major barrier to success.

Imagine that you work for a non-profit environmental organization. With a grant from a major utility company, you sign a contract to run $1 million worth of ads on cable TV encouraging people in your city to reduce their home energy use. Excited to be able to reach so many people, you begin to think about exactly how you should word the ads. What should the script be like? What sort of messaging should you use to get people to listen and to act? What approach will be most likely to persuade people to reduce their home energy use?

Because you're not sure, you reach out to colleagues at some other environmental non-profits to ask them. What you hear back just leaves you more uncertain. One friend tells you to focus on global warming and the effects it will have on people's daily lives if we all don't cut back on our energy use. A staffer at another environmental organization suggests you focus on the harm that coal-fired power plants are doing to wildlife, since a lot of people in your city enjoy watching wildlife in the local parks. A third colleague encourages you to focus on the air pollution and asthma generated by energy production, since people are likely to empathize with the plight of sick kids. A fourth says that, if you really want to be effective, you have to get people thinking about how much money they can save by cutting down on their energy use.

All of these ideas and explanations sound very reasonable. You could certainly see any of these messages working well with your audience. But you start to wonder: "I know these are full-time staffers who do nothing but work to protect the environment, but do any of them really know which message is most effective at getting people to cut back on their energy use? Or are they like the children in Amanda Waterman's study, taking their best guess based on the limited information they have instead of giving the honest answer, 'I don't know.'"

Unless your colleagues had scientific testing to point to in support of their beliefs about which message works best—and, as you quickly learn, none of them did—all they were doing was guessing. While their guesses may have been thoughtful, reasoned, and with anecdotal evidence to back them up ("This is what convinced my neighbor to start using less energy"), they were still guesses. Neither they nor you have any idea about which message really works best.

Since none of your colleagues really know what works best, you decide to carry out some testing to see which message is most effective at persuading people to reduce their home energy use. You create a set of five advertisements that look very similar but that have different messaging about why to reduce energy use. Using an inexpensive online survey platform, you recruit people to come and view your ads and then state whether and how they plan to reduce their home energy use in the next month. By also gathering their email addresses and phone numbers, you're able to follow up with them a month later to see whether or not they actually reduced their energy use.

What you find from your experiment is that ad number four turned out to work 20 percent better than any of the others. People reduced their home energy use 20 percent more when they were shown ad number four compared to when they were shown one of the other ads. Now that you know what works best, you put the DVD with ad number four in an envelope, seal it up, and send it off to the cable company so they can begin running your ad. Mission accomplished!

Increasing the effectiveness of a program by 20 percent may seem like a minor improvement, something not worth the hassle of creating and testing different ads. But that improvement has about the same impact for the environment as getting 20 percent more money into your budget. Since your grant for television ads was $1 million, that means doing the testing had nearly $200,000 worth of value! That's a heck of a lot of value for one little test.

Because of that, even in the unlikely scenario that it cost you a whopping $150,000 to design, test, and measure the impacts of the five different ads, it would have been worth it. You would still have reduced more home energy use than if you had not bothered to carry out the test and had instead spent the full $1 million on ads.

That is the value of testing and measurement. The 20 percent figure is just a hypothetical example. Many tests will turn up larger variations in impact among different programs or different approaches. One website layout might be 35 percent more effective than another at generating donations for Greenpeace. A homeless shelter might find it costs 80 percent less per person housed when they focus on housing families instead of individuals. The Seva Foundation might find it costs 50 percent less to identify, treat, and cure a person of blindness in India than it does in Bangladesh. Measuring and acting on such data could allow these organizations to raise more money, house more homeless people, and cure more cases of blindness.

Sadly, in testing to figure out which approach would work best before launching your television ads, you would be in relatively virgin territory in the non-profit world. Right now, guesses and assumptions remain the lifeblood of most charity work. Non-profits typically decide which approaches to use based on a haphazard mix of personal philosophy, past precedent, anecdotal evidence, and speculative reasoning. Donors and volunteers operate mainly from guesses as well.

Consider, for example, the following two questions:

1. How much money has been spent trying to alleviate global poverty?
2. How much money has been spent testing to see how effective different interventions are at alleviating global poverty?

Many billions of dollars were spent on the former before a single penny was spent on the latter. To spotlight just one type of intervention as an example, hundreds of millions of dollars have been spent by the anti-poverty organization Heifer International (HI) to provide animals to people in developing countries. Yet, HI has not done any scientific testing to see how effective giving away animals is compared to other possible interventions. They haven't even tested to make sure that giving away animals does more good than harm. Of course, HI is just one example of an organization putting the cart before the ... er, heifer. It's only in the past few years that testing has begun to be done on any anti-poverty programs, including programs as simple as directly giving money to poor people.

When it comes to charitable work, we sometimes consider questions like "What is the best way to alleviate global poverty" or "Which message will be most effective at persuading home owners to reduce their home energy use?" as questions of opinion or philosophy. Actually, they are questions of fact. They have concrete answers. If we don't know the answers, it's because we haven't taken the time to test and find out, or we haven't taken the time to look at the results of testing others have already done.

This is true for the big questions, such as how to prevent homelessness. It's also true for a myriad of smaller questions that non-profit staffers must answer on a daily basis. For example, which website design will enable us to collect the most new email signups? Which types of social media posts should we put out if we want them to be shared as widely as possible? Is it better for us to run paid advertising on television, online, or on the radio to promote our next event? Which demographic audience is most likely to respond to and become involved with our cause?

For most non-profit staffers, the instinctual response to questions like these is much like those of the children in Amanda Waterman's study, the baseball scouts in the days before Billy Beane, and the campaign managers in the years before Big Data: to take a guess based on experience and reasoning. But guesses will often be wrong; only testing and data can tell us the real answers.

Testing will always be imperfect, and the results of one study can't give us an ironclad guarantee that one method is better than another. But as long as the studies are designed well, the results will be correct more often than not. That probability alone makes them incredibly powerful and worthwhile. Plus, the more direct testing we do, the more certain we will be. While no single test can perfectly account for every variable, we should not use that as an excuse to avoid trying something new, putting in the work of testing, and being willing to be proved wrong.

Some non-profits and foundations are starting to catch on. For example, the 2013 *Gates Letter*, an open letter to supporters of The Bill and Melinda Gates Foundation from its chairman, Microsoft Founder Bill Gates, centered around one central theme: that testing is absolutely vital to success in the non-profit world. "I have been struck again and again by how important measurement is to improving the human condition," writes Gates (Gates, 2014).

As another example, the Abdul Latif Jameel Poverty Action Lab (J-PAL), founded in 2003 in the Economics Department of the Massachusetts Institute of Technology, carries out randomized control trials to see how effective poverty reduction and disease prevention campaigns are. In one study J-PAL tested to see whether it was better to give away anti-malaria bed nets for free or to charge a very small price for them. The study found that giving the nets away was more effective at preventing the spread of malaria. Thanks to J-PAL's research, health agencies are now able to make more effective decisions when trying to combat this disease.

Here's one final example of the power that research and testing can play in bringing about a better world. In 2008 marriage equality groups suffered a painful defeat with the passage of Proposition 8 in California, a referendum that banned same-sex marriage in the state. Afterward, the non-profit group Freedom to Marry conducted dozens of focus groups around the country to understand why their side had failed and how they could successfully rebound in the 2012 election cycle. Through split-testing various advertisements and messages, they were able to determine which wordings and which sound bites were most effective at persuading those who were on the fence about or mildly opposed to marriage equality to begin supporting it.

They learned, for example, that talking about "fairness" was more effective than talking about "equality." They learned that discussing "marriage" or the "freedom to marry" was more effective than using terms like "gay marriage" or "same-sex marriage."

And they learned that showing images of long-term committed gay couples doing the typical things married couples do, such as mowing the lawn or helping an elderly neighbor, was more effective than framing the issue around "rights" (Ball, 2012).

With an updated playbook in hand and volunteers rigorously versed in the dos and don'ts of advocating for marriage equality, Freedom to Marry dove into battle in 2012 in support of a statewide referendum in Maine that sought to legalize same-sex marriage. Despite the challenges of persuading a rural, aging, and heavily Catholic population to support marriage equality, Freedom to Marry and its supporters were victorious at the polls. Maine became one of the first states in the country to legalize gay marriage at the ballot box.

To succeed, Freedom to Marry—and marriage equality advocates in general—had to come to terms with three things. First, that the messaging they were using to advance their cause was not succeeding. Second, that they did not know which messaging would work best. Third, that the only way to find out what would work best was through direct testing.

It's only after we admit how much we don't know that we can start to replace our guesses with research and data and become more successful at the work we're doing. While we'd like to think we have all the answers, we should view how much we don't know through a positive lens. If we already knew everything, there would be no way for us to improve and accomplish more good. The more we realize what we don't know, the more space we have to learn and improve. Every new question mark is a new opportunity to make the world an even better place, as long as we take the time to find the answers.

10

NINE STEPS TO GREATNESS

Throughout this book we've looked at the hurdles we face in trying to be great at doing good. While the hurdles are real, they're actually pretty easy to overcome. Think of them as six inches tall, barely jutting above the ground but hard to spot in the tall grass. Because we don't notice them, they trip us up again and again. Jumping over them is the easy part. The hard part is noticing they're there and recognizing them for what they are: obstacles that get in the way of doing good.

Does it take a healthy dose of attention to spot them every time? Sure. Does it take some self-discipline to always jump over them? Sure. But it's something every one of us can do. Succeeding at charity doesn't take an inordinate amount of time, money, or energy. We don't have to be incredibly smart. We don't have to be the hardest worker. We don't have to be the most compassionate or the most passionate person. Obviously, all of these can help us be more effective, but we can do an incredible amount of good for the world without being superhuman.

Here in summary are nine steps to being great at doing good. If we want to make the world a better place—if we want to, in the words of Schindler, "get more out"—consider this a roadmap for how to do it. If it sounds at times like tough love, that's exactly what it is. We are all intelligent adults, and we can be frank with one another about what works and what doesn't. If it sounds at times like a pep talk, that's exactly what it is, too. Every one of us could stand to get fired up again about making the world a better place.

Here, then, are nine steps to being great at doing good. Get ready to truly change the world for the better!

1. Get Serious

If we want to succeed at charity, we have to first get serious about it. We may not feel the same emotional intensity for our work that players in a football locker room feel just minutes before the Super Bowl, but we should have the same determination to win that every one of them has, if not more. There is so much more on the line with whether or not we succeed in our charity work than there is with whether or not the team succeeds at winning the big game. Lives are at stake. Intense suffering is at stake.

We need to be truly driven to win. The people in any field who are consistently successful are those with a day-by-day, hour-by-hour obsession with achieving. The field of charity is no exception. There is nothing more serious than the problems we are trying to solve, so we should be seriously committed to solving them. If we don't have a driving hunger to succeed, then we aren't treating charity with the seriousness it deserves.

2. Never Forget the Goal of Charity

If we are serious about charity, then we need to burn into our brains exactly what the goal of charity is. Without it, we're like a driver without a destination. We don't know where we're going, so at every intersection we have no idea which way to turn.

The goal of charity is to *reduce suffering and increase well-being as much as possible.* In other words, the goal of charity is to make the world as much of a better place as possible. Every decision should be made with that goal in mind.

When we don't base our decisions around that goal, we are being guided not by altruism but by some personal motivation. Charity should not be about us. It is not about what we want, what we enjoy, or what we are drawn to. It is not about feeling good or proving we're good people. It is about reducing as much as possible the very real suffering of others that occurs just outside our sights.

The goal of charity is crystal clear. The challenge is keeping that goal in mind at all times and having the self-discipline to base our charity decisions around it.

3. Shun Fuzzy Thinking and Feel-Good Rhetoric—They Are Self-Centered

Far too often, we think of the goal of charity as "doing good." We love this goal because it's easy. It gives us a permission slip to forego critical thinking. It permits us to continue doing what we've already been doing and what we find enjoyable. It lets us fail without feeling like we failed. It pats us on the head and tells us we're winners just for taking part.

When we have a fuzzy goal like "doing good," we see improving the world a tiny bit as no different from improving the world a whole lot. It leads us to ignore the fact that choosing to do one thing means choosing not to do another much more important thing. It shields us from having to admit that some charitable programs are thousands of times more effective than others.

This sort of thinking, and the feel-good rhetoric that comes with it, are inherently self-centered. They make internal intentions, and not real-world results, central in importance. They make us feel better about ourselves in the short term, but the rest of the world pays the price.

Thankfully, there is a powerful antidote to all of this, and that is to maintain a rigid insistence on basing charity decisions around one single question: "What will improve the world the most?"

4. Be Aware of the Psychological Biases We All Have

We all have psychological biases. We respond to causes that push our emotional buttons or that give us an emotional reward for being involved. Because of that, we're more likely to respond to crises than we are to work for systemic change that prevents problems from happening in the first place. We are more likely to donate to causes that intersect with our own lives and that are geographically close to home. We are more likely to donate to individuals than we are to groups, and more likely to donate when we hear stories than when we hear statistics. We focus on human problems, even when donating to other issues—such as helping animals or protecting the environment—has the potential to reduce vastly greater amounts of misery.

Psychological biases don't just shape the choices of donors; they shape the choices of volunteers and non-profit staffers as well. We are more likely to do charity work that we find personally enjoyable. We are more likely to do work that doesn't require significant sacrifice. We are more likely to do work for which we can see the results up close and personal.

Each of these speaks to our biggest bias of all: our bias toward ourselves. We're hard-wired to want to do what's best or easiest for us, not what's best for the cause we support. This can lead us to favor mild benefits to ourselves over massive benefits to those we are trying to help.

All of these biases have been carved into our brains by the forces of evolution. We can't change the fact that they exist. But the more we recognize them for what they are, the less power they will have to steer us in the wrong direction. The more we notice them when they pop up, the more we'll be able to work around them and make smarter charitable decisions. At times we can even put our self-centeredness to work, harnessing our drive to achieve and using it to accomplish even more good for the world.

5. Be Willing to Face the Hard Facts

If we're serious about charity and honest with ourselves, we'll soon come face-to-face with some surprising facts. For example, we'll realize that some programs and organizations are thousands of times more successful at doing good than are others in the same field. We'll realize that certain charity fields will always be hundreds of times more effective at improving the world than others. We'll also realize that succeeding at charity requires making calculated decisions about who to help and who to ignore. How much we succeed at charity will depend in large part on how willing we are to accept these facts and act accordingly.

This can be very hard to do. It requires a willingness to see our own shortcomings and to dramatically change what we're doing when the numbers tell us to—two things that we are not inclined to do. If one hundred donors to the Theater Communications Group read this book, how many do you think would change what they were doing and start donating to Seva or another charity instead? Probably just a few. Most would hold on to what they felt was some good reason for continuing to donate to TCG. The same would happen with donors to any less-successful group. And if most donors would be unwilling to face the hard facts and change, just imagine the likely reaction of staffers at TCG and other less-efficient charities.

This is the problem. When our habits, intelligence, and sense of goodness are called into question, we are all little Einsteins at finding ways to justify our current choices. We ignore the hard facts. When we can't ignore them, we question those facts. When we can't question the facts, we question how much those facts matter.

Like any other form of self-honesty, we are either willing to face the hard facts or we are not. We either have the self-discipline to act on them or we don't. If we don't, we have little chance of truly succeeding at the goal of charity.

As threatening as they may initially seem, we should actually cherish and appreciate the hard facts. While they might turn our current charitable approach on its head, they teach us that success can be surprisingly easy if we look for it in the right place. They show us how we can accomplish even more good for the world than we're accomplishing now. In that way, they empower us to do exactly what it is we want to do: make the world an even better place.

6. Define and Make Decisions Around a Bottom Line

Whatever charitable field we work in, we have to define a key metric to measure our success. This is our personal bottom line, our cost per good done. For most non-profits, the bottom line will be pretty straightforward: cost per animal saved, cost per homeless person housed, cost per hungry child fed, and so forth. Organizations that run a variety of programs might have multiple bottom lines.

Taking a bottom-line approach requires that we temporarily reduce the unique individuals we're trying to help to numbers. That doesn't mean we don't care about them; quite the opposite. It's because each individual is so valuable that we want to help the greatest number of individuals possible. That's why focusing on the bottom line is so important. It tells how and where we can help the most individuals.

Once we've defined our bottom line, we need to base all our decisions around it. If our bottom line is cost per sick child helped, what can we do to lower that cost and thereby help more sick children? Are there other non-profits that have a lower cost per sick child helped and, if so, how can we copy what they're doing? Are there certain programs we carry out that have a higher cost per sick child helped than our other programs? If so, we need to eliminate or at least cut back on those programs and shift the extra money toward ones with a low cost per sick child helped. A willingness to shift course when the numbers tell us to is a hallmark of strength and intelligence.

Much like Dorothy following the yellow brick road, we need to follow the bottom line wherever it takes us, even if that may be to some pretty unexpected places. Once we've defined our bottom line and committed to basing all decisions around it, we have a clear path to continual improvement. All we need to do is follow the path, turning when the bottom line tells us to turn and going straight when the bottom line tells us to go straight.

7. Measure, Measure, Measure

We often assume we know which approaches work best for achieving the goals of our charitable causes. The reality is that, much like the children in Amanda Waterman's study, we're usually just guessing. We don't know the answer, so we make one up based on our intuition and anecdotal evidence.

The only real way to know which approach works best is to test different approaches and measure the results. That takes work. It means spending time, money, and energy designing and carrying out the research and analyzing the results. Not only does it take work, but it also seems to lack a sense of urgency. Because of that, many non-profit staffers see measurement as a distraction from their "real" work. A common sentiment is that, while it would be nice to have that sort of information, it's more important to spend time and money on direct programming than on measuring the programming that's being done.

This sounds reasonable, but it's not. Imagine you were driving across the country and your engine went screwy a few hours into the trip. You could no longer drive over forty-five miles per hour without the engine overheating. What would you do? Would you continue the rest of the drive at forty-five miles per hour, since you were in too much of a hurry to stop and fix the engine? Or would you stop at an auto garage to have the engine fixed? That would mean spending a few hours sitting idle, but it would ultimately take you across the country much more quickly.

Like stopping to fix the engine, measuring the impact of different approaches has a small up-front cost and a big long-term pay-off. We will never know how much more effective we can be unless we take the time to measure what we're doing and test different alternatives. While this isn't always possible, it usually is.

Although it can take some work and resources, it's often worth the effort. Every opportunity for testing and measurement is an opportunity to become more efficient at making the world a better place. We should take full advantage of that opportunity whenever we can.

8. Give Non-Profits the Incentive to Be Great

If you donate to charity, ask non-profits for hard numbers on exactly what they're achieving. What is their cost per good done? What is the cost per good done of other organizations you could donate to instead?

Poverty reduction organizations should be asked how many individuals they help out of poverty per dollar donated. Health organizations should be asked how many lives they improve per dollar donated. Animal protection organizations should be asked how many animals they help per dollar donated.

Having this information can help us figure out which organizations will do the most good with our money. By supporting the most efficient groups, we also incentivize the charity field as a whole to focus on what really matters: improving the world as much as possible. If non-profits know that having a high cost per good done will cause them to lose donors, they will work hard to lower that cost.

There is one problem with this: most non-profits don't have data to share. Only a small percentage of non-profits measure the impact they're having. We should favor organizations that do collect and share that sort of data, since it allows us to be more certain of the impact our donations will have. If we're making a large donation, we can even earmark it toward the group's most effective program.

By focusing our donations on the organizations with the lowest cost per good done, we can both accomplish an incredible amount of good and help create lasting change in how charity is carried out.

9. And Remember: Never Forget the Goal of Charity

Yes, we are repeating ourselves. But the point is so crucial that it bears repeating: never forget the goal of charity.

The goal of charity is to make the world a better place. Charity is not about feeling good, looking good, living out our passion, expressing our beliefs, making our lives more enjoyable, or anything else having to do with us. The same goes for charitable organizations. Their goal is not looking good, raising money, occupying a certain niche, maintaining a positive public image, or anything else that has to do with the non-profit itself. Sometimes these things overlap with the goal of charity. Many times they don't.

There is an unfathomable amount of very real misery and suffering going on just outside the borders of our comfortable lives. Every charitable decision we make should be based on one question and one question only: Which choice will reduce as much of that suffering as possible?

Conclusion
The Joy of Great Charity

Now that you've worked your way through this book, doing good might seem a lot more complicated than it used to. It may feel like something simple and enjoyable has been turned into an unpleasant chore.

The fact is that making the world a better place is a challenge. Compassion and kindness will accomplish relatively little on their own. Only when we add in self-awareness, critical thinking, and mental discipline will we be able to truly succeed at bringing about the change we want to see.

All challenges seem intimidating at first. When we're sitting on the couch eating potato chips, the idea of getting up to go running along cold winter roads seems intimidating and extremely unpleasant. But once we do it, once our feet hit the pavement and we've passed our first couple of blocks, things change. Once we commit, there is exuberance in testing ourselves against the challenge before us. There is deep pleasure in learning, improving, persevering, and achieving.

This is as true for charity as it is for running or any other challenge. And when it comes to charity, there is also something breathtakingly beautiful on the other side. The amount of good that each one of us is able to do in our lifetimes is absolutely staggering.

Recall from earlier that the Seva Foundation spends less than a hundred dollars for every person it spares from the misery of blindness. Some of the best farmed animal protection organizations spend less than a dollar for each animal—an animal as smart, unique, and playful as the cat or dog we lovingly dote on at home—that they spare from a lifetime of suffering. If we are smart, calculated, and committed in our approach to charity, we can do a truly incredible amount of good: sparing hundreds of people from blindness or sparing tens of thousands of animals from a lifetime of pain are just two examples.

These are the sorts of things that every one of us can accomplish if we approach charity with the seriousness and rigor it deserves. Is there anything else we could achieve in our personal or professional lives that even comes close in importance? Is there any better use of our time, money, or energy than working to achieve these sorts of changes?

None of us wants to look back later in life with Schindler's regret, realizing only too late that we could have "got more out," that we could have helped end the very real suffering of so many more individuals around the world but failed to do so. The good thing is, we don't have to.

When World War II ended, so did Schindler's unique opportunity for saving the lives of Jewish workers. But for you and me, our opportunity to do great things remains as long as we're alive to walk this earth. We can dive back into charity work tomorrow with renewed vigor and a new focus on doing as much good as possible. Not only can we bring about incredible change in the lives of others, but we can do so while experiencing the joy and exuberance of tackling this work head on.

Are you up for the challenge?

About the Author

Nick Cooney is director of education at Mercy For Animals and founder of The Humane League. He is also the author of *Change of Heart: What Psychology Can Teach Us About Spreading Social Change* and *Veganomics: The Surprising Science on What Motivates Vegetarians, from the Breakfast Table to the Bedroom*. He has lectured extensively across the United States and Europe on how to carry out charity effectively, and his work has been featured in hundreds of media outlets, including *TIME* magazine, *The Wall Street Journal*, and National Public Radio.

References

Anderson, Jack. "W. McNeil Lowery Is Dead; Patron of the Arts was 80."
    The New York Times. June 7, 1993. www.nytimes.com/1993/06/07/
    obituaries/w-mcneil-lowry-is-dead-patron-of-the-arts-was-80.html.

Ball, Molly. "The Marriage Plot: Inside This Year's Epic Cam-
    paign for Gay Equality." *The Atlantic.* December 11, 2012.
    www.theatlantic.com/politics/archive/2012/12/the-marriage-plot-
    inside-this-years-epic-campaign-for-gay-equality/265865/.

Charity Navigator. "Giving USA 2008, The Annual Report on Philanthropy."
    Charity Navigator. March 1, 2010. www.charitynavigator.org/index
    .cfm?bay=content.view&cpid=42.

Collins, James C. (2001). *Good to Great: Why Some Companies Make the
    Leap—and Others Don't.* New York, NY: HarperBusiness.

Collins, James C. (2005). *Good to Great and the Social Sectors: A Monograph to
    Accompany Good to Great.* New York, NY: HarperCollins.

Freakonomics. "The Three Hardest Words in the English Lan-
    guage: Full Transcript." *Freakonomics.* May 15, 2014.
    http://freakonomics.com/2014/05/15/the-three-hardest-words-in-
    the-english-language-full-transcript/.

Fritz, Joanne. "Examples of Effective Fundraising Letters." About.com. Octo-
    ber 1, 2014. http://nonprofit.about.com/od/fundraising/ss/Examples-
    Of-Direct-Mail-Fundraising-Letters_4.htm.

Gates, Bill. "Annual Letter 2013." The Bill & Melinda Gates Foundation.
    October 1, 2014. www.gatesfoundation.org/Who-We-Are/Resources-
    and-Media/Annual-Letters-List/Annual-Letter-2013.

Heath, Chip, and Dan Heath. (2013). *Decisive: How to Make Better Choices in
    Life and Work.* New York, NY: Crown Business.

Hope Consulting. "Money for Good." Hope Consulting. October 1, 2014.
    www.hopeconsulting.us/moneyforgood.

Kennedy, John F. "I Am a Berliner." Public Speech, West Berlin, Germany,
    June 26, 1963.

Landman, Anne. "Front Group King Rick Berman Gets Blasted
    by His Son, David Berman." *PR Watch.* January 30, 2009.

www.prwatch.org/news/2009/01/8168/front-group-king-rick-berman
-gets-blasted-his-son-david-berman.

Lewis, Michael. (2003). *Moneyball: The Art of Winning an Unfair Game*. New
York, NY: W.W. Norton.

Merriam-Webster. "Charity." *Merriam-Webster Dictionary*. October 1, 2014.
www.merriam-webster.com/dictionary/charity.

Rumsfeld, Donald H. "DoD News Briefing–Secretary Rumsfeld and
Gen. Myers." U.S. Department of Defense. February 12, 2002.
www.defense.gov/Transcripts/Transcript.aspx?TranscriptID=2636.

Spielberg, Steven, Steven Zaillian, Liam Neeson, Ben Kingsley, Ralph
Fiennes, and Thomas Keneally. (1994). *Schindler's List*. Universal
City, CA: MCA Universal Home Video.

Wikipedia. "Vince Lombardi." Wikipedia. October 1, 2014. http://en
.wikipedia.org/wiki/Vince_Lombardi.

Wikiquote. "Joseph Stalin." Wikiquote. October 1, 2014. http://en.wikiquote
.org/wiki/Joseph_Stalin#Misattributed.

Williams, Greg. "Larry Williams Is Humanity's Best Hope Against the Next
Pandemic." *Wired*. May 14, 2014. www.wired.co.uk/magazine/archive.

Index